THE ESSENTIAL
MANIFESTING
GUIDEBOOK 2022

THE ESSENTIAL
MANIFESTING
GUIDEBOOK 2022

Simple Steps To Create
The Life You Truly Desire

TRISH MCKINNLEY

7th STAR
PUBLISHING

DAYTON, OH

Trish McKinnley/7th Star Publishing
251 W. Central Ave, Suite 140,
Springboro, OH/USA 45458-6057

Ordering Information:
Quantity sales. Special discounts are available on quantity purchases by corporations, associations, and others. For details, contact the "Special Sales Department" at the address above.

The Essential Manifesting Guidebook 2022/ Trish McKinnley. —1st ed.
ISBN 978-1-7333015-2-7 (paperback)

*To all the dreamers who know
there's more to life and are ready to manifest it.*

*And to my husband, Jim,
who made my dreams come true!*

ACKNOWLEDGEMENTS

To the amazing goddesses who helped manifest this book!

Molly Wendell for the rapid late-night editing, holding my hand, guiding, and giggling.

Karen Kay for your encouragement, design help and understanding chocolate is a priority.

Kelsey Schaub for listening and organizing the chapters as only a magical Virgo can!

Carol McIntosh for understanding donuts, wine and sweet tart ropes.

Joy Palmer who believes in me, sharing laughter until we cry!

Angie Kline for your magical sparkle and understanding of Diet Coke.

Jesse Smart for holding down the fort.

Hazel Morales for your smile, magic and prayers.

Tonya Kappes for getting this whole thing started when she said, "DO THE BOOK!"

And all the magical members in Fairydust 101 and Goddessology.

Thanks for sharing this journey!

May your dreams be manifested before you even ask.

XOXOXO

CONTENTS

Introduction

There's magic in the air. It seems we all notice that "something." Even if we connect just for a split moment, we know it's there. Then we notice the moon, especially on a full moon night. We comment how it makes people more emotional. We look at the stars and suddenly remember the poem, Star Light Star Bright. Unless you're like me and can only recall the first stanza. I don't know about you, but I always skip ahead to the important part—making my wish. We've been tapping into the cosmic energies for making our dreams come true forever! Literally. Our ancestors scribbled all about it on the cave walls.

Fast forward to today and we have apps for checking the heaven's happenings so we can up-to-date on our horoscope and when we need to prep for the next dreaded cycle of Mercury Retrograde. See? You intuitively know the value of the heavens. You sense the guidance.

This book is the compilation of cosmic guidance, giving you access to the amazing and brilliant energy and influence, enabling you to deliberately work with their wisdom. To not just make a wish but to manifest our wish come true.

This guidebook is split into sections for easy-to-find reference. You can employ as many or as few of the cosmic manifesting energies as you want. In the front you'll find the 2022 calendars with all the cosmic events. So, decide what you want to manifest. Look at the calendar for the current cosmic manifesting opportunities Read about each in their corresponding section for their manifesting tips and energies. Choose how you want their help.

Let's Talk Manifesting

You're probably already knowledgeable on manifesting. However, please read through this so you're able to connect with my meanings and methods. My students and clients have manifested love, houses, dream jobs, cars, unexpected income and babies faster than they ever thought possible. This works.

Some of the manifesting steps you'll read include paper, pencils, and colored pencils. These are really pencils. These are not to be substituted for pens, crayons or markers. The lead in the pencils are closest to the natural energy of the earth. This works best for manifesting.

And, you don't have to take my word for it. My student, Melani, took my vision board class two years in a row. The first year she used what she had— crayons. The next year she used pencils. She told me, "I had success with the first. It was slow, but my dreams did manifest. I used pencils this time. The next day, I got offered a new job. The very next day!"

The Golden Rule of Manifesting

You can't force someone else to do your bidding. Free will and all. You can manifest. You do it all the time. You are a natural. I know this. However, I can't manifest for you. As much as I'd love to, it's all about you. You can do this.

Manifesting 101

The goal of this Essential Manifesting Guidebook is to guide you through making the most of the manifesting energies throughout the year. To provide the knowledge so you can set yourself up for success. Ride the wave. Join the movement. There is a flow. Think about the cycle of the sun. Energy is all around. Ride this wave of energy. You just have to know the wave. You can start at any time. Use it anytime of the year.

Maybe life is great in January. Yay! I'm celebrating with you. Then this is great context for being in the know of the cosmic energies. Then, suddenly you have an amazing dream, like you want to buy a new car or get in better shape for bikini season. Great! Go to the current month, read up on the cosmic energies, decide how you want to apply, and ride that manifesting wave.

Manifesting starts... and ends with you. To manifest, you need three key elements:

1. The Mindset
2. Your Vibe
3. Taking Action

The Mindset

What are you thinking? Are you feeling like the little engine that can? Thoughts are key here. And some of your mindset is the natural influence of your astrological sign. If you know your sign is a natural glass half-full then lean into that. Find that silver lining even more. And, if you're not that sign, then make the most of every day the sun is in that sign and when a cosmic event is occurring within that sign.

Mindset is the first key to manifesting. If you're thinking it'll never happen for you then you're right. If you're thinking of course that can happen for you... right again!

Your Vibe

Your vibration is the signal you're naturally radiating to the world. It's your personal broadcasting signal. This is the lighthouse for the desire.

For example: You want love. You're beaming love and love is coming. Then, you have an argument and your mindset slips into feeling unworthy and thoughts of *who am I kidding?*

Next, your light dims. Your vibration went from zinging to sluggish. There's a reason. Low, negative thoughts produce low and slow energy. High, positive thoughts produce high and fast energy. Low creates weak signal. High creates powerful signal.

How do you know where your vibe is? It has to do with your feelings.

1. How are you feeling?
2. What interactions are your experiencing?

Feelings

You know your feelings. To keep it simple just categorize as high, neutral or low. High is the love, gratitude, joy, appreciation. Neutral is "meh." Low. It's anxious, sad, overwhelmed. In order to manifest what you want, begin at least in the neutral zone. You'll be able to nudge it up to high.

It's as easy as stepping into nature or literally turning that smile upside down. Yep. Just smiling will shift your vibe.

Interactions

You know the interactions you're having. Are you having positive conversations? Are you encountering frustrations? It's telling. Identify the overall theme and you'll have confirmation of your vibe. Your vibe dips. Your light dips. Good vibes only baby!

Taking Action

You've got to create momentum. Make the call. Write the text. State the affirmation. Just like nothing happens to the seed in the ground. It has to wiggle through the dirt and reach out. You've got to do some movement too. And, just reading this book you've begun "shimmying through the dirt."

Keep taking internal action making sure your thoughts and vibe are staying in the ideal manifesting zone. Now, trust your intuition and divine guidance and take outward actions. Explore. Meditate. Smile back at the sun. Take the actions in this book. Take the action letting the universe know you mean business and you will manifest that dream.

MANIFESTING TIP: *When manifesting apply the FIT Method. Focused. Intentional. Thought.*

When things begin to slide or not seem to be on course, go back to your thoughts. When a frustration occurs, and it does because you're human and living your life, definitely stay FIT. Staying FIT means asking yourself, "Are these thoughts aligned with my intentions or are they distracting me?"

For example: You're a single mom manifesting your soul mate. Your thoughts are "I am aligned with love. My soul mate loves me!" Then, some well-meaning co-worker says, "no one wants to marry someone with kids" or even worse, Baby Daddy says, " Who'd want to marry you?" Ugh. Words. They carry a vibration.

And that vibration just tried to derail your thoughts and high vibe. But wait! Yay! Words! It's okay because you're going to stay FIT. *Focused Intentional Thought.*

Entertaining any of the thoughts of unworthiness or filling with fear or doubt is not staying focused on your intention of finding a soulmate. Those negative thoughts planted by the co-worker and Baby Daddy do not align with your desire. They must be thrown out. And return your thoughts to your intention. Double down baby!

"I *am* manifesting my soulmate!"

"I *am* worthy of my soulmate."

"I have more soulmates than I know what do with."

Okay, maybe the last one is extreme, but you get the idea. When negative thoughts or encounters occur, ask if it's aligned with your focused intentional thought. You already intuitively know the answer. If not, release it. Return to your focus.

Don't you dare let that negative intrusion distract you. Stay FIT.

Using this Book

1. Identify what you want to manifest.

2. Consult the calendar and get the cosmic happenings.

3. Decide which events you want to use for manifesting and create your plan. Suggestions accompany each cosmic event. You can pick from those or choose your own. Just, please do something. Your dreams are worth it!

For example:

1. You want to manifest more money.

2. Your FIT (focused intention thought) is to manifest money.

3. Download the Monthly Cosmic Energy Plan.

4. Flip to January's Month Page for the month's happenings and calendar.

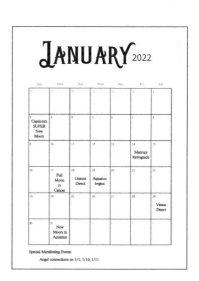

5. You see Astrological signs are Capricorn and Aquarius. There is a Capricorn Super New Moon, Full Moon in Cancer and another New Moon in Aquarius. You note there are currently 2 retrogrades Uranus and Venus which will be going direct. And, Mercury will be retrograding.

6. Find the moon cycle information in the moon chapters, the retrograde information in the planet chapters and the astrology sign information in the astrology chapter.

7. While reading each cosmic manifesting energy, decide how you want to apply to your manifesting intention of making more money.

Capricorn is hard-working and a planner and can help you create the steps and fortitude to manifest. Aquarius can provide out-of-the-box ideas.

The two New Moons can bring new seeds of income.

Uranus and Venus going direct giving me options. Mercury is going retrograde so I'm going to make sure I'm communicating clearly.

Month _____

I am Manifesting _____

_____

Cosmic Manifesting Energies: Page #

Astrological Signs -

_____   _____

New Moon

_____   _____

Full Moon

_____   _____

Other events to note. (Retrogrades, cosmic events)

                                                              F.I.T.

Manifesting energies I want to apply

_____

_____

My action plan -

_____

_____

_____

_____

_____

_____

_____

_____

Essential Manifesting

MONTHLY COSMIC ENERGY PLAN

Month _____January_____

I am Manifesting   *More money*
_____

_____

Cosmic Manifesting Energies: Page #

Astrological Signs -
_____*Capricorn & Aquarius*_____   _____

New Moon -
in Capricorn on 2nd & Aquarius on 31st   _____
_____

Full Moon -
in Capricorn on 2nd & Aquarius on 31st   _____
_____

Other events to note - (retrogrades, cosmic events)

Uranus & Venus go direct, Mercury goes Retrograde

                                                             F.I.T.

Manifesting energies I want to apply -

Venus Retrograde, Uranus going direct, New Supermoon in Capricorn and | *I am attracting and receiving an abundance of money.* |
_____

My action plan -

Print my calendar download included in my bonus from buying the book.

Use Venus to remember when money seemed to flow and to remind myself that I'm worthy.

Apply Uranus advice to expect the unexpected to stay manifesting money. Do a 3 moon manifesting tips.

_____

_____

_____

_____

ESSENTIAL MANIFESTING

A full-size version of the Monthly Cosmic Energy Plan is included as your bonus for purchasing the book. To access, go to my website **www.trishmckinnley.com/book** *and put in your order number. The downloads will be readily available.*

Manifesting
WITH THE
Months

★

*Each month brings specific
manifesting energy and focus.
This section outlines the dates so you
can plan your manifesting accordingly.*

Months and Their Manifesting Energies

E very month holds manifesting magic. This year is off to a great start! We enter this year in the midst of retrogrades. There's so much in store for you in 2022 and it's so much easier when you know how to plan ahead.

Elements for each month are covered in this section:

- *Calendar.* This is an at-a-glance of the current month.

- *Astrology Sign.* For the manifesting influences. Refer to the Astrology chapter for more details on each sign.

- *Moon Cycle.* For the manifesting influences and details refer to the Moon Section and chapters.

- *Cosmic Events.* These include retrogrades, eclipses, unique days like equinoxes, solstices, and gateways. Refer to the Planets chapter for more detail on manifesting with the retrogrades. Refer to the Cosmic Events chapter for more details on manifesting with the rest of the cosmic events.

NOTE: *All times listed are US Eastern Time. Please check for your local time. I like the website https://www.timeanddate.com.*

JANUARY 2022

Sun	Mon	Tue	Wed	Thu	Fri	Sat
26	27	28	29	30	31	1
2 Capricorn SUPER New Moon	3	4	5	6	7	8
9	10	11	12	13	14 Mercury Retrograde	15
16	17 Full Moon in Cancer	18 Uranus Direct	19 Aquarius begins	20	21	22
23	24	25	26	27	28	29 Venus Direct
30	31 New Moon in Aquarius	1	2	3	4	5

Special Manifesting Events

Angel connections on 1/1; 1/10; 1/11

JANUARY 2022

———

MANIFESTING ENERGY: New beginnings, Working with Angels

SIGN: Capricorn/Aquarius

MANIFESTING EVENTS:

This month begins with 2 planets in retrograde,
Uranus until the 18th and Venus until the 29th.

Mercury will Retrograde from the 14th January to 3rd February
1, 1/10, 1/11 bring heightened angel communication

NEW MOON IN CAPRICORN*
Supermoon
2 January 1:33 pm

FIRST QUARTER
9 January 1:11 pm

FULL MOON IN CANCER
17 January 6:48 pm

LAST QUARTER
25 January 8:40 am

NEW MOON IN AQUARIUS
FOR SOME
1 February 12:46 am

FEBRUARY 2022

Sun	Mon	Tue	Wed	Thu	Fri	Sat
30	31	1 New Moon in Aquarius	2	3 Mercury Direct	4	5
7	7	8	9	10	11	12
13	14	15	16 Full Moon in Leo	17	18 Pisces begins	19
20	21	22	23	24	25	26
27	28	1	2	3	4	5
6	7	8	9	10	11	12

Special Manifesting Events

Chinese New Year of the Tiger Begins 1 February

New partnerships with spirit guides, especially fairies on 2/2

FEBRUARY 2022

———

MANIFESTING ENERGY: Mystical, Loving, Partnerships

SIGN: Aquarius/Pisces

MANIFESTING EVENTS:

This month begins with Mercury retrograde,
however quickly goes direct on the 3rd.

1 February Chinese New Year Begins. This is in the Year of the Tiger.

2/2 brings new partnerships with spirit guides: angels, fairies,
ascended masters, goddesses, power animals, mermaids.

For some, there will be NO new moon in your area for the month of
February as it will occur on January 31. This is significant. This occurs
every 19 years. The 1 brings the energy of wholeness, new beginning,
your soul. The 9 represents a completed cycle. Think back 19 years
ago. What were you doing? What did you want? What dreams have
manifested in that time? What dreams have you forgotten? What new
dreams were birthed from this time? What new beginnings would
you like to infuse into this New Moon cycle? This will be a powerful
manifesting new cycle wherever you're celebrating this New Moon.

NEW MOON IN AQUARIUS*
1 February 12:46 am

FULL MOON IN LEO
16 February 11:56 am

FIRST QUARTER
8 February 8:50 am

LAST QUARTER
23 February 5:32 pm

MARCH

2022

Sun	Mon	Tue	Wed	Thu	Fri	Sat
27	28	1	2 New Moon in Pisces	3	4	5
7	7	8	9	10	11	12
13	14	15	16	17	18 Full Moon in Virgo	19
20 Aries begins Equinox	21	22	23	24	25	26
27	28	29	30	31 New Moon in Aries	1	2
3	4	5	6	7	8	9

Special Manifesting Events

Heightened energy to work with ascended masters 3/3

MARCH 2022

———

MANIFESTING ENERGY: Powerful & Gentle, Good Luck, Swift Shifts

SIGN: Pisces/Aries

MANIFESTING EVENTS:

There are NO retrogrades during this month.

The Equinox occurs on the 20th. This is the Spring for the northern hemisphere and the Fall Equinox for the southern hemisphere.

3/3 brings heightened ascended masters energy

NEW MOON IN PISCES
2 March 12:34 pm

FULL MOON IN VIRGO
18 March 3:17 am

FIRST QUARTER
10 March 5:45 am

EQUINOX
20 March

LAST QUARTER
25 March 1:37 am

 2022

Sun	Mon	Tue	Wed	Thu	Fri	Sat
27	28	29	30	31	1	2
3	4	5	6	7	8	9
10	11	12	13	14	15	16 Full Moon in Libra
17	18	19 Taurus begins	20	21	22 Uranus Direct	23
24	25	26	27	28	29 Pluto Retrograde	30 New Moon in Taurus Eclipse
1	2	3	4	5	6	7

Special Manifesting Events

Angel energy on 4/4

APRIL 2022

———

MANIFESTING ENERGY: Beauty, Love, Fertility

SIGN: Aries/Taurus

MANIFESTING EVENTS:

No retrogrades until the end of the month when Pluto goes retrograde on the 29th. Pluto will go direct October 8th.

Partial Solar Eclipse at the end of the month!

4/4 brings heightened angel energy.

NEW MOON IN ARIES*
1 April 2:24 am
(This is one of those occasions where some will have the New Moon the day before. You can set your New Moon intentions either day.)

FIRST QUARTER
9 April 2:47 am

FULL MOON IN LIBRA
16 April 2:55 pm

LAST QUARTER
23 April 7:56 am

NEW MOON IN TAURUS*
30 April 4:28 pm
*This is also a Solar Eclipse (Partial) Solar influence the outer (taking action, impacting outward change, manifesting outward abundance) Eclipses brings swift and powerful change. Wish wisely!

MAY 2022

Sun	Mon	Tue	Wed	Thu	Fri	Sat
1	2	3	4	5	6	7
8	9	10 Mercury Retrograde	11	12	13	14
15 Scorpio Full Moon Eclipse	16	17	18	19	20 Gemini begins	21
22	23	24	25	26	27	28
29	30 New Moon in Gemini	31	1	2	3	4
5	6	7	8	9	10	11

Special Manifesting Events

Power day for welcoming change on 5/5

MAY 2022

———

MANIFESTING ENERGY: Fertility, Celebration, Blooming

SIGN: Taurus/Gemini

MANIFESTING EVENTS:

Pluto is retrograde until 8th of October

Mercury goes retrograde on the 10th until 3 of June

Lunar Eclipse this month!

5/5 power day for welcoming change

NEW MOON IN TAURUS*
Solar Eclipse
Cycle began
30 April 4:28 pm
This is also a Solar Eclipse (Partial)
Solar influence the outer (taking action, impacting outward change, manifesting outward abundance) Eclipses brings swift and powerful change. Wish wisely!

FULL MOON IN SCORPIO
Lunar Eclipse
16 May 12:14
*Lunar Eclipse (Total)
This is also a Lunar Eclipse (Total) Lunar influence the inner (trusting intuition, impacting inner change, manifesting emotional breakthroughs) Eclipses brings swift and powerful change.

FIRST QUARTER
8 May 8:21 pm

LAST QUARTER
22 May 2:43 pm

NEW MOON IN GEMINI
30 May 7:30 am

JUNE 2022

Sun	Mon	Tue	Wed	Thu	Fri	Sat
29	30	31	1	2	3 Mercury Direct	4 Saturn Retrograde
5	6	7	8	9	10	11
12	13	14 Sagittarius SUPER Full Moon	15	16	17	18
19	20	21 Cancer begins Solstice	22	23	24	25
26	27	28 Full Moon in Cancer Neptune Retrograde	29	30	1	2
3	4	5	6	7	8	9

Special Manifesting Events

Harmony and balance is brought on 6/6
Solstice on the 21

JUNE 2022

———

MANIFESTING ENERGY: Vitality, Romance, Joy

SIGN: Gemini/Cancer

MANIFESTING EVENTS:

Planets in Retrograde are Pluto, until the 8th October
and Mercury until the 3rd of June.

Saturn is going retrograde on the 4th of June until the 23rd of October.

Neptune is going retrograde on the 28th of June
through 3rd of December.

This month celebrates a solstice on the 21st! This is the
Summer Solstice for the northern hemisphere and
the Winter Solstice for the southern hemisphere.

6/6 brings an energy of harmony and balance.

NEW MOON IN GEMINI*
Cycle began
30 May 7:30 am

LAST QUARTER
20 June 11:10 pm

FIRST QUARTER
7 June 10:48

SOLSTICE
21 June

FULL MOON IN SAGITTARIUS*
Supermoon
14 June 7:51 am

NEW MOON IN CANCER*
28 June 10:52 pm

JULY 2022

Sun	Mon	Tue	Wed	Thu	Fri	Sat
26	27	28	29	30	1	2
3 Sirius Gateway Begins	4	5	6	7 Sirius Gateway Ends	8	9
10	11	12	13 Capricorn SUPER Full Moon	14	15	16
17	18	19 Chiron Retrograde	20	21	22 Leo begins	23
24	25	26 Lionsgate Gateway Begins	27	28 New Moon in Leo Jupiter Retrograde	29	30
31	1	2	3	4	5	6

Special Manifesting Events

Energy of attainment is brought on 7/7
Sirius Gateway 3 July through 7 July

JULY 2022

———

MANIFESTING ENERGY: Independence, Spiritual, Personal Power

SIGN: Cancer/Leo

MANIFESTING EVENTS:

Planets in Retrograde are:

Pluto, until the 8th October

Saturn until the 23rd of October

Neptune until the 3rd of December

Chiron retrogrades 19th July until 23 December

Jupiter retrogrades 28th July until 23 November

Sirius Gateway occurs this month and the Lionsgate Gateway begins.

There's a full supermoon.

7/7 Attainment

NEW MOON IN CANCER*
Cycle began
28 June 10:52 pm

FULL MOON IN CAPRICORN*
Supermoon
13 July 2:37 pm

SIRIUS GATEWAY
3 July – 7 July

LAST QUARTER
20 July 10:18 am

FIRST QUARTER
6 July 10:14 pm

LIONSGATE GATEWAY
26 July – 12 August

NEW MOON IN LEO
28 July 1:54 pm

$\mathcal{A}$UGUST 2022

Sun	Mon	Tue	Wed	Thu	Fri	Sat
31	1	2	3	4	5	6
7	8 Lionsgate Portal	9	10	11 Aquarius SUPER Full Moon	12 Lionsgate Gateway Ends	13
14	15	16	17	18	19	20
21	22 Virgo begins	23	24 Uranus Retrograde	25	26	27 New Moon in Virgo
28	29	30	31	1	2	3
4	5	6	7	8	9	10

Special Manifesting Events

Mega Manifesting 8/8
Lionsgate Portal 8/8
Lionsgate Gateway ends 12/8

AUGUST 2022

———

MANIFESTING ENERGY: Manifesting, Harvest, Gratitude

SIGN: Leo/Virgo

MANIFESTING EVENTS:

This is a month full of manifesting. The vibration of the month is an 8! We enter this manifesting month in the flow of Lionsgate Gateway with Lionsgate portal occurring on the 8th.

Planets in Retrograde are:

Pluto, until the 8th October

Saturn until the 23rd of October

Neptune until the 3rd of December

Chiron retrogrades 19th July until 23 December

Jupiter retrogrades 28th July until 23 November

Uranus retrogrades 24 August until 22 January 2023

There's a Full Supermoon and 8/8 Mega manifesting

LIONSGATE GATEWAY	LIONSGATE PORTAL
26 July – 12 August	8 August
NEW MOON IN LEO*	FULL MOON IN AQUARIUS
Cycle began	11 August 9:35 pm
28 July 1:54 pm	
	LAST QUARTER
	19 August 12:36 am
FIRST QUARTER	
5 August 7:06 am	
	NEW MOON IN VIRGO
	27 August 4:17 am

ȘEPTEMBER 2022

Sun	Mon	Tue	Wed	Thu	Fri	Sat
28	29	30	31	1	2	3
4	5	6	7	8	9 Mercury Retrograde	10 Full Moon in Pisces
11	12	13	14	15	16	17
18	19	20 Uranus Direct	21	22 Libra begins Equinox	23	24
25 New Moon in Libra	26	27	28	29	30	1
2	3	4	5	6	7	8

Special Manifesting Events

Heightened goddess energy 9/9

SEPTEMBER 2022

———

MANIFESTING ENERGY: Goddess Energy, Transformation, Growth

SIGN: Virgo/Libra

MANIFESTING EVENTS:
The Equinox occurs on the 22nd. This is the Fall for the northern hemi-sphere and Spring Equinox for the southern hemisphere.
9/9 brings heightened goddess energy
Planets in Retrograde are:
Pluto, until the 8th October
Saturn until the 23rd of October
Neptune until the 3rd of December
Chiron until 23 December
Jupiter until 23 November
Uranus until 22 January 2023
Mercury goes retrograde 9th September until 2 October

NEW MOON VIRGO*
Cycle began
27 August 4:17 am

FIRST QUARTER
3 September 2:07 pm

FULL MOON IN PISCES
10 September 5:59 am

LAST QUARTER
17 September 5:52 pm

EQUINOX
22 September

NEW MOON IN LIBRA
25 September 5:54 pm

OCTOBER

2022

Sun	Mon	Tue	Wed	Thu	Fri	Sat
25	26	27	28	29	30	1
2 Mercury Direct	3	4	5	6	7	8 Pluto Direct
9 Full Moon in Aries	10	11	12	13	14	15
16	17	18	19	20	21	22 Saturn Direct
23 Scorpio begins	24	25 New Moon in Scorpio Solar Eclipse	26	27	28	29
30 Mars Retrograde	31	1	2	3	4	5

Special Manifesting Events

This is a manifesting month. Octo is Latin for 8.

Heightened energy for manifesting new on 10/8, 10/10, 10/18

OCTOBER 2022

———

MANIFESTING ENERGY: Magical, New Beginnings & Endings, Manifesting

SIGN: Libra/Scorpio

MANIFESTING EVENTS:
This month is also a powerful manifesting energy. "Octo" is derived
from the Latin word for 8. The 10 brings endings and new beginnings.
10/8, 10/10, 10/18 for manifesting new.
The veil begins to thin this month until fully exposed on the 31st.
This is a time for celebrating our ancestors, communicating with spirit
guides such as angels, fairies and ascended masters.
Plus, there is a partial solar eclipse.
Planets in Retrograde are:
Mercury goes direct on the 2nd October
Pluto, goes direct the 8th October
Saturn until the 23rd October
Neptune until the 3rd December
Chiron until 23rd December
Jupiter until 23rd November
Uranus until 22 January 2023
Mars retrogrades on the 30th until 12 January 2023

NEW MOON IN LIBRA*
Cycle began
25 September 5:54 pm

FIRST QUARTER
2 October 8:14 pm

FULL MOON IN ARIES
9 October 4:54 pm

LAST QUARTER
17 October 1:15 pm

NEW MOON IN SCORPIO*
Solar Eclipse
25 October 6:48 am

NOVEMBER 2022

Sun	Mon	Tue	Wed	Thu	Fri	Sat
30	31	1	2	3	4	5
6	7	8 Full Moon in Taurus Lunar Eclipse	9	10	11	12
13	14	15	16	17	18	19
20	21	22 Sagittarius begins	23 New Moon in Sagittarius Jupiter Direct	24	25	26
27	28	29	30	1	2	2
4	5	6	7	8	9	10

Special Manifesting Events

Angel connections on 11/1; 11/11

NOVEMBER 2022

———

MANIFESTING ENERGY: Gratitude, Angels, Abundance

SIGN: Scorpio/Sagittarius

MANIFESTING EVENTS:
This month is packed with angel blessings.
1/1, 1/11 for easy angel communication
There is a lunar eclipse this month!
Planets in Retrograde are:
Neptune until the 3rd December
Chiron until 23rd December
Jupiter until 23rd November
Uranus until 22 January 2023
Mars until 12 January 2023

NEW MOON IN SCORPIO*
Cycle began
25 October 6:48 am

FIRST QUARTER
1 November 2:37 am

LAST QUARTER
16 November 8:27 am

FULL MOON IN TAURUS*
*Lunar Eclipse
8 November 6:02 am
*This is also a Lunar Eclipse
(Total) Lunar influence the inner
(trusting intuition, impacting inner
change, manifesting emotional
breakthroughs) Eclipses brings
swift and powerful change.

NEW MOON IN SAGITTARIUS
23 November 5:57 pm

DECEMBER 2022

Sun	Mon	Tue	Wed	Thu	Fri	Sat
27	28	29	30	1	2	3 Neptune Direct
4	5	6	7 Full Moon in Gemini	8	9	10
11	12 Merkaba Gateway Begins Merkaba Portal	13	14	15	16	17
18	19	20	21 Merkaba Gateway Ends Capricorn begins Solstice	22	23 Capricorn SUPER New Moon Chiron Direct	24
25	26	27	28	29 Mercury Retrograde	30	31
1	2	3	4	5	6	7

Special Manifesting Events

Merkaba Gateway begins 12/12
Merkaba Portal 12/12
Merkaba Gateway ends 12/21

DECEMBER 2022

MANIFESTING ENERGY: Divine Guidance, Vibrational Increase, Transformation

SIGN: Sagittarius/Capricorn

MANIFESTING EVENTS:
There is a new Supermoon!
Retrogrades for the month -
Neptune goes direct 3rd December
Chiron goes direct 23rd December
Uranus until 22 January 2023
Mars retrogrades on the 30th until 12 January 2023
Mercury retrogrades 29 th December until 18 January 2023
12/12 through 12/21 is the Merkaba Gateway
12/12 is the Merkaba Portal
This month celebrates a solstice on the 21st! This is the Winter Solstice for the northern hemisphere and the Summer Solstice for the southern hemisphere.

NEW MOON IN SAGITTARIUS*
Cycle began
23 November 5:57 pm

FIRST QUARTER
30 November 9:36 am

FULL MOON IN GEMINI
7 December 11:08 pm

MERKABA PORTAL
12 December

LAST QUARTER
16 December 3:56 am

SOLSTICE
21 December

NEW MOON IN CAPRICORN*
Supermoon
23 December 5:16 am

FIRST QUARTER
29 December 8:20 pm

Manifesting
WITH THE
Cosmic Events

★

*Cosmic events occur throughout the year bringing
specific energy, alignment and manifesting shortcuts.
Every event provides a spiritual upgrade.
Deliberately choosing to access these events
will help accelerate manifesting.*

Meanings & Manifesting

The universe is powerful. It's always in motion. And that motion can help or hinder us. It's up to you to decide how to let the universe affect you.

Cosmic events covered in this section:

- *Equinox* happens twice a year. The sun is over the equator creating equal amount of day and night. Spring and Fall.

- *Solstice* happens twice a year. The sun is farthest from the equator creating the longest and shortest day of the year. Summer and Winter.

- *Solar Eclipse* is when Earth slips into the moon's shadow.

- *Lunar Eclipse* is when the moon slips into Earth's shadow.

- *Gateway/Portals* are spiritual openings for advancements. These times provide spiritual tune-ups, upgrades and enhancements, thus making manifesting easier.

  > *Sirius Gateway* is an annual event when our sun's older, big brother, Sirius is closest to Earth. Sirius is known as our spiritual sun.

> *Lionsgate Gateway/Portal* is an annual event when manifesting is markedly escalated.

> *Merkaba Portal* is a time for upgrading your vibration with the Divine Light. This portal opens on the 12th of December and completes its upgrade on the Winter Solstice.

- *Retrograde* is when the planet appears to be going backwards. This is a time used for revealing, remembering and reviving. Retrograde dates are included in this chapter, while manifesting with each planet's retrograde is included in the planet chapter.

Use These Cosmic Events

Cosmic events bring an escalated and powerful surge of energy. Actually, you don't even have to do anything to benefit. You will receive a positive vibrational boost just from the event.

For manifesting, review the purpose of each and how to incorporate into the outcome you want.

1. Identify how you wish to use the event.
2. Work through these steps or create your own manifesting routine.

Spring Equinox

S pring Equinox is the time of year when the day is the same length as the night. Talk about balance! The energy of new growth, rebirth and awakening is happening in nature and within our homes. What would you like to welcome in and manifest into your during this season of hope, fertility and growth? You can plant seeds, walk in nature, and do stretches or yoga. This is also a natural time for spring cleaning and preparing your home for new manifesting energies.

How to Use the Spring Equinox

1. Clean your sacred space. A sacred space is a room, bedside table, windowsill. You may have trinkets or objects with a divine connection, a candle, or even nothing. The intention is this area is designated for your intimate, spiritual connection.

    By cleaning your area you're wiping away all stagnant, old and stale energy. *Please don't panic or feel like you have to lug out a mop and gloves! When I don't have time for a proper cleaning, I just wave my hand over the space.*

    Set your intention for this space to be completely cleared of the old and energized with the new. This space is a fresh start like the fresh earth in Spring.

2. Grab paper, pencil, colored pencils, red candle and matches. We're going to make an egg mandala!

3. Draw a large egg on the paper. Egg is the symbol for life. This represents the dream you're ready to manifest.

4. Within the egg, draw the outcome you desire as if it's already attained. This is a focused space for your manifestation to Spring forth.

MANIFESTING TIP: *Hand draw this image. Do not print out an image. This is to come from you as part of YOUR creation. You do not need to be an artist. You just need to set the intention for what you draw to come true.*

5. Add colors to empower your egg. Just like color therapy is used today, ancients knew the energy of color, which is why many people color eggs during Easter.

6. Once you feel your egg is complete, place your drawing in your sacred space.

7. Light a red candle.

8. Looking at your egg mandala, state your intention....

   "Today I celebrate the energy of a new cycle in the world and within me. I welcome the sun and fulfillment of the desires placed in my egg. I choose to and will take action to manifest this treasure that is aligned with my soul's path. It is with my sincerest gratitude that I welcome and honor this cycle of growth."

9. Extinguish your candle and place it by your paper. Know this red candle is like a magnet calling out to the universe and all the spiritual assistance. It says "notice me!"

10. Take a moment visualizing this image as it has manifested! Really lean into the emotions of joy, success and gratitude.

11. When you feel ready, thank your angels for providing encouragement and guidance for this manifestation.

"I am fresh like spring attracting fresh new blessings."

Fall Equinox

Fall Equinox is the other time of year when the day is the same length as the night. Another powerful time for balance! The energy of harvest, gratitude, abundance, balance and new seeds. Just like the acorns that are snuggling into the ground, ready to grow into a humongous oak tree, this is a mighty manifesting time.

How to Use the Fall Equinox

1. *Celebrate your harvest.* Write down all of your successes for this year. Use front and back. This is a time of celebrating the cornucopia of overflowing blessings. Include your accomplishments. Any progress or growth is important. Remember that little acorn. It seems tiny, but that little nut on the ground is the beginning. Boast about your every accomplishment! This can be something as simple as saying a daily affirmation!

2. *Balance.* Draw a circle representing your favorite pie. Divide the pie into slices representing how much time, including thoughts, energy and action, is dedicated to each of the following: home, family, friends, self, work, and dreams. Are there areas out of balance that may need tweaking prior to planting the new manifesting seeds?

3. *New seeds.* Identify what new seeds to plant.

4. *Gratitude.* This is a time of celebrating the cornucopia of overflowing blessings.

Release and Let Go

With the good, sometimes bad has infiltrated. This can be negative thinking, feeling disheartened or just an "out with the old, in with the new" desire.

1. Title your paper with List 1 and write a list of what needs to be released. *For example: painful memories, hurts, insecurities, doubt, misunderstanding, regrets, that thing that happened 7 years ago.*

2. On a fresh page, title it List 2 and write what you desire. *For example: dreams, goals, creating new memories, financial security, peace of mind.*

3. Find a safe place to burn your lists. (I have an iron pot with a lid for indoor burning and a specific firepit for outdoors exclusively used for these types of things.)

4. Burn List 1 saying, *"Thank you for the experience & knowledge gained. I no longer need nor benefit from holding onto these lessons. If there is still more to be understood for my soul, I will attract it in a kinder, loving way. I bless and release all attachments, identities and limitations. Thank you!"*

5. Allow burning of the list to complete before the next step.

6. Burn List 2 saying, *"Thank you for igniting these dreams & desires. I am open to receiving blessings & love for my highest good. I allow the energy of love and success to radiate from my soul. With harm to none. Thank you!"*

7. Safely ensure the fire is extinguished. Do not roast marshmallows over these ashes. Wash your hands as a signal to the Universe that you know it's acting on these desires.

"I am blessed every day, in every way."

Summer Solstice

*S*ummer Solstice is the longest day of the year. Ancient civilizations celebrated the summer solstice. Even to this day there are activities and festivals. All of this fuels the manifesting energies. It's literally kindling for the manifesting bonfire. This is a time to activate your intentions, soak in the healing power of the sun and the positive manifesting energies. This day holds sizzling energy of action, passion and manifesting success. Ask yourself, "What do I truly want to manifest?"

A Summer Solstice Manifesting Ritual

1. Set your alarm to wake prior to sunrise.

2. Grab paper, pencil, colored pencils and your favorite morning beverage. *I intentionally bring my sun tea for this special morning.*

3. Snuggle into a cozy place where you'll be able to see the rising sun.

4. As the sun rises, begin creating your manifesting vision sheet.

   Draw images of what you want to manifest. Use symbols or sketch images to the best of your abilities. For example, a heart for love or a treasure chest full of coins and jewels or a smiley face representing joy for successfully manifesting all that you desire.

   Write on your page, *"Thank you for this or something better."*

5. Once the sun is fully shining, hold your sheet and stand. Still holding your sheet, raise your arms as if soaking up the morning rays and pulling in her energy.

6. Thank God and the angels for the sunshine, creating a clear path and for overseeing your dreams come true.

   You can say something like, *"Thank you for blessing my dreams. I honor and appreciate the heightened energy flowing to my desires during this powerful time. Thank you, God, and angels for accelerating the manifestation of these dreams fulfilled. As always, my sincere desire is for harm to none and blessings for all. Amen."*

7. Leave your paper where it will energize in the sun all day.

"I am radiant and beaming with manifesting energy."

Winter Solstice

Winter Solstice is the shortest day of the year. Even though daylight will begin to increase daily, this is a time of going within, reconnecting with our inner flames and blanketing ourselves with confidence.

A Winter Solstice Manifesting Ritual

(To empower this ritual, listen to my Winter Solstice Guided Meditation on my YouTube channel or website trishmckinnley.com)

SUPPLIES NEEDED:
Yellow or gold candle
Paper, pencil and colored pencils

1. Light your candle.

2. Draw a large rectangle on your page.

3. Within the rectangle, create a table with 9 squares by drawing 2 horizontal and 2 vertical lines within. Just like a tic tac toe within the rectangle.

4. In the boxes draw the following symbols: evergreen tree, mistletoe & holly, star, sun, candle, snowflake, and draw a present with a bow in each of the 3 remaining squares.

5. Add color in your symbols.

   Red for strength, protection and good luck

   Green for protection prosperity and mental rejuvenations

   White for this new magical, manifesting phase, new goals and new sense of peace and bliss

   Silver for increased healing, increased clarity and heightened intuition

   Gold for accelerated success, increased abundance and happiness.

6. Thank God and the angels for the warmth and every glowing flame. You can say something like, *"Thank you for wrapping my dreams and desires in the warm, loving protection. I am filled with peace and gratitude knowing these dreams have already come true and are just waiting to come to light. I honor and appreciate the manifesting energy flowing to my desires during this powerful time. Thank you, God, and angels for accelerating the manifestation of something better or these dreams fulfilled. As always, my sincere desire is for harm to none and blessings for all. Amen."*

7. Using your candle to light the way, place this in your sacred space. Extinguish your candle and place the candle on or by your sheet.

   "I am a beautiful and powerful light"

Eclipse

LUNAR & SOLAR

Eclipses deliver powerful and accelerated change. They pinpoint what's blocking our success in manifesting. They aren't stingy with the information either. If you ask, they will tell you. Eclipses used to cause panic and fear as the moon or sun disappeared. The light provided by the heavenly bodies gets blocked and the sky gets dark. To this day, animals still get disoriented. There is no need for you to be concerned, though. You can intuitively sense the upcoming event and simply allow the adjustments to play out in your life. You can also choose to plan around the event and make the most of this rapid impact.

- Eclipses come in pairs.

- Eclipses provide laser focus.

- A solar eclipse only occurs with a new moon, so it will always usher in an impactful new beginning.

- Eclipses occur two to three times a year.

- A *Solar Eclipse* is when Earth slips into the moon's shadow. The line-up is earth, moon, sun.

- A *Lunar Eclipse* is when the moon slips into Earth's shadow. The line-up is moon, earth, sun.

How does this impact manifesting?

Solar Eclipse Energy for Manifesting

Use the energy of the solar eclipse for physical and external changes and taking actions. When working with the solar (sun) energy, explore all things associated with the sun: exertion, masculine energy, decisiveness, reactive, demonstrative, outgoing.

Lunar Eclipse Energy for Manifesting

Use the energy of the lunar eclipse for emotional and spiritual changes and upgrades. Remember, lunar (moon) energy is connected with intuition. Its feminine energy is receptive, introspective, and intimate. The lunar eclipse pinpoints thoughts and fears that are hindering your manifesting success. Each eclipse occurs in an astrological sign. The sign's energy delivers its concentrated influence for revealing manifesting blockages too.

Navigating Eclipses

Prior to the eclipse:

1. Note the current time for your location. I like the website *www. timeanddate.com*

2. Note the astrological sign for the eclipse and characteristics. Would you like to leverage this sign's energy?

3. Identify where you'd like clarification. You'll know this area because you're already experiencing frustration around this.

4. Write your list and set it aside. For example, *"What's blocking me from financial abundance? What's blocking the love of my life? What's with this extra weight?"*

5. Throughout the day look for the revelations. You may suddenly notice signs and symbols appearing. Pay attention to this guidance. Your intuition will help identify, acknowledge and interpret the messages you receive.

6. Next you get to decide how you want to proceed. Do you acknowledge but choose to ignore? Do you commit to taking action and welcome in the transformations? Whatever you decide is perfect for you. If you want to move forward, then commit to three ways you will implement the epiphanies the eclipses provided.

7. Offer words of gratitude for the clarity. Take a cleansing breath.

Shifts will continue after the eclipse, so keep noticing the divine guidance of signs, symbols, and messages.

2022 Eclipse Dates

30 April 04:42 pm ET	New Moon in Taurus | Solar Eclipse
15/16 May 00:12 am ET	Full Moon in Scorpio | Lunar Eclipse
25 October 07:01 am ET	New Moon in Scorpio | Solar Eclipse
8 November 06:00 am ET	Full Moon in Taurus | Lunar Eclipse

How to Work with the Solar Eclipse in Taurus

Taurus is dependable, practical and loyal. They have an appreciation for the finer things. Their good taste is rivaled only by their beauty – inside and out. They are a manifesting magnet. Digging their heels in this Earth sign is going to manifest what she wants. The new moon energy with Taurus is influential in manifesting new paths, beginnings and insight in finances, love and projects that will be long-lasting. Use this eclipse to discover what's blocking you from achieving these.

Are you taking the wrong actions? Are you focused on the wrong priorities because you're doing what you think you should be? Are you trying to do things perfectly and end up not doing anything? The Solar Eclipse will bring this to light so you can make adjustments. Work with this manifesting shift. You'll see the progress by 8th of November and the full moon in Taurus Lunar Eclipse.

How to work with the Lunar Eclipse in Scorpio

The moon brings the emotions and the water sign, Scorpio, does too! A key strength of this eclipse is intuitively receiving the guidance.

This is wonderful for exploring your soul's depth and discovering what's keeping you from your passion. Write in your journal before the 16th of May.

1. Identify where you're harboring fear and do a Release Ceremony. Do you have deep seated fears and insecurities around money, manifesting, worthiness, relationships or beliefs?

2. Does your emotional or spiritual routine need evaluating? Perhaps it's time to include meditation into your daily routine or explore working more with crystals. Maybe a new routine includes grounding yourself or putting a protective bubble or incorporating simple smudging.

How to work with the Solar Eclipse in Scorpio

New moon energy brings new beginnings, new starts and new energies. Scorpio brings the passion, intensity and even reveals the secrets of your heart! Connected with your sacral chakra. This is perfect timing for revealing where you can take manifesting action in the areas of intimacy, relationships, creativity, sexuality, and your emotions.

Trust your intuition. Are you feeling emotionally disconnected from what you want to manifest? Do you want to manifest something you're passionate about or it's what someone else wants? Are you feeling inept and not the confident soul you truly are? Are you feeling blocked from your intuition?

To manifest anything, two elements are a must. Intuition. Confidence. Both come from deep within you. Scorpio and this new moon provide a fresh, new start. Recommit to yourself and your dreams. This may seem like a silly exercise, but it works. Do the figure 8 with your hips while stating your affirmation.

"Every day in every way I am attracting my desires."

How to work with the Lunar Eclipse in Taurus

Use this eclipse to discover what's blocking you from manifesting, especially in love and finances. This full moon will shed the light and the lunar eclipse is going to bring the swift change. Grab your journal and identify what needs to change. Write your commitment to welcoming and embracing this change.

Taurus is ruled by the Goddess Venus who brings victory. She even makes you more fertile in your manifesting. This is the time to work with her! In Mind. Body. Spirit.

Mind

Are you affirming success or doubt? Are your thoughts fueling success? Are you spending 17 seconds a day visualizing success? After the eclipse, write a new affirmation. State it aloud. Visualize victory.

Body

Are you taking action? Are you trusting your intuitive guidance? After the eclipse, ask your intuition for three things to do that'll help you manifest faster. Do this by closing your eyes and taking a cleansing breath. Ask your divine self, "What can I do to manifest this desire?" Open your eyes and begin writing. When you feel like you have a complete plan, write on your paper, "I commit to this" and sign and date.

Spirit

When was the last time you did some spiritual self-care? This is a perfect time to grab your sage stick and smudge yourself. You can watch my video on my YouTube channel or on my website www.trishmckinnley.com). Search on *sage cleansing yourself.*

Sirius Gateway
3 JULY - 7 JULY

This an annual event when our sun's older, big brother, Sirius is closest to Earth. Sirius is known as our spiritual sun. Just like our sun strengthens us physically and the moon strengthens us emotionally, Sirius strengthens us spiritually.

This gateway is a time of independence. When manifesting are there topics that provide freedom in your life? Occurring in the sign of Cancer, your intuition will be heightened. Trust the messages communicating from your sixth sense. Logic will try to talk you out of manifesting before you even get started, so tune in and allow your intuition to be your guide.

Use this time for manifesting!

1. What do you want brought into your life?

    For example, abundance of love, money health? Fertile ground for pregnancy, creativity or opportunities? Rebirth in self-confidence, self-care or in those dreams buried so deep?

2. Based on your answer(s) above, write out each desire in a positive affirmation as if you've already achieved this.

    For example: You desired several options above, your affirmation may be "I am receiving all that I desired." Let's say you desired peace-of-mind, then your affirmation could be, "Every day in every way I am healthier, happier and more confident."

3. Sirius Gateway is an elevated time to work with spiritual guides.

Choose one of the 3 ways to use this guidance.

CALL ON ANGELS

> Ask your guardian angel for assistance

> Ask Archangel Barachiel for guidance in success, prosperity and abundance

> Ask Archangel Jeremial for help being strong and finding the new, positive path

There are many more angels, if you feel led to call on another.

When calling on angels, talk to them just like you're speaking with a dear family member. They already intimately know and love you. No need to be formal. You can keep it simple like saying, *"Archangel Barachiel, please help me."*

CALL ON FAIRIES

> Talk to Daisy Fairies for easy communication and a positive outcome

> Talk to Light Fairy to illuminate the best path to manifest faster and best outcome

> Talk to Lavender Fairy for total peace and quick healing

Call on fairies to help align with Sirius Gateway's elevated energy and vibrations. When communicating with fairies, speak aloud in nature. Trust your intuition for their replies. You may sense a message or experience a feeling of joy. Fairies are communicating!

CALL ON THE GODDESS OF SIRIUS, GODDESS SOPDET

> When manifesting new starts, new beginnings and new light to shine on your dreams

> When you need increased productivity or growth

> When you need help releasing and trusting the outcome

Goddess Sopdet is the brightest star in the Canis Major constellation. She signaled the start of the new year and is a symbol of fertility. When communicating with her go out each night. Try to find her star. It's okay if it's cloudy or you don't have time to locate her. Speak aloud and make your request known. Close your eyes and imagine her loving light shimmering down upon you. Trust the messages you intuitively sense. Thank her.

You can continue working with Goddess Sopdet even after this gateway.

Each day apply your manifesting checklist.

MORNING:

- Imagine your successful day prior to getting out of bed.
- State your affirmation 3 times and every time you pass a mirror.
- Stay alert to the spiritual messages provided throughout the day.
- Take action.

EVENING:

- Write 3 things you noticed during the day
- Write 3 things you're grateful for.
- Spend 7 minutes visualizing and feeling the joy of having already accomplished your dreams.

This manifesting daily habit can continue throughout the year!

Journal insights and manifesting wins. Even if you're manifesting stronger intuition, this is something to celebrate! You are claiming your soul's independence and the freedom to achieve the life you desire.

"I am free to attract and receive all good things."

Lionsgate Gateway

Lionsgate Gateway is an annual event beginning the 28th of July until the 12th of August with the portal occurring at the zenith of manifesting. The date of 8/8 is significant in regards to both numerology and astrology. When on its side, the 8 makes the infinity sign. This symmetry of this number brings balance to your material and immaterial world. And! This wonderful, powerful number aligns and manifests abundance and financial prosperity.

Lionsgate Gateway occurs during the astrological sign of Leo. Leo energy boosts feminine energy, and brings more creativity, nurturing and intuition. This lion energy will give you the courage to pursue your dreams and will teach you balance, patience and sexiness.

This entire gateway is a time of receiving vibrational uploads, boosts and increases. You'll notice through dreams, intuition and signs you receive. These aren't by mistake. These are intentional gifts for your encouragement.

Use this 8/8 for manifesting!

1. Set your intention. I know you've read this repeatedly, but by setting your intention, the universe opens and connects you with endless possibilities to support your intention. I usually set this intention, *"It is my intention to soak up the energy boost of Lionsgate Portal to use as I desire throughout the rest of the year."*

(If you aren't sure what intentions to set, you can grab my intention setting worksheet here at www.trishmckinnley.com/intentionsettingworksheet/)

2. Sit in the Sun.

    Go outdoors and sit in the sunlight absorbing this transformative manifesting energy. You can apply sunscreen, wear a hat, just be in the sun, for 8 minutes. Be confident that as you bask in the sun you ARE clearing away the blockages and receiving and attuning to the higher manifesting and spiritual frequency. You can enjoy the energy in quiet or add a meditation like my Lionsgate Portal Meditation on YouTube.

3. If need be, you can continue this step in the shade. Now that you're feeling supercharged, and maybe a little sleepy, it's time to write. In your journal, write what you intend on manifesting. This is a great opportunity to stretch yourself. Go bigger. This is the time to explore manifesting
    - Miracles
    - Overcoming hurt
    - Attracting love of your life
    - Creating an app
    - Writing a book
    - Releasing anything blocking your peace
    - Stepping into your power
    - Being heard
    - Feeling and knowing you're desirable
    - Anything your intuition is sharing

    Complete this sentence in your journal. "It is my intention to manifest..." Begin each sentence this way.

4. Look over your sentences and read each one aloud, changing the words from, "it is my intention to..." to "I am a manifesting magnet for..."

For example, "It is my intention to manifest being a successful speaker at a TED talk" becomes, "I am a manifesting magnet for being a successful speaker at a TED talk."

Read these new sentences aloud. Use your strong voice. Roar like the lion. As you're speaking these, feel the truth of your statement. When you've finished with your list, conclude with, *"I align with the confidence and courage to receive these or something better."*

5. Time to daydream or take a catnap! Spend another 8 minutes daydreaming that these have manifested. Give each sentence its due attention. This is a precious time as you are working alongside the magic of the Lionsgate Portal, Sirius, Goddess Sopdet and your guardian angel. You are loved and meant to have dreams come true.

"I am powerful."

Merkaba Portal

This annual event occurs every December. Beginning on the 12th and concluding on the Winter Solstice. Whether we are intentional or not, we do receive a spiritual upgrade, with healing energies, clearer angel guidance and a stronger vibrational signal. By recognizing the significance and the power of this portal, we have an opportunity to step into our soul's greater love and brighter light.

Merkaba is an ancient Hebrew word that's actually a compilation of three separate words.

> *Mer - Light*
> *Ka - Spirit*
> *Ba - Body*

Your Merkaba field extends beyond your aura field. This is where your soul's destiny blueprint resides. This is where you have a clearer, greater, and easier connection with the Divine. What upgrade would you like? Clearer intuition? Healing? Peace? Confidence in your manifesting? Quicker manifesting connection? Stronger angel connection? Don't know?

How to Use the Merkaba Portal

Know what you want to manifest.

Set your timer for 12 minutes.

Get comfortable and close your eyes. Imagine yourself in the center of the Star of David, also known as a 6-pointed star or star tetrahedron.

Imagine yourself sitting or standing as you visualize golden flecks of light swirling around you. Each is filled with energy, love, and a divine connection.

Imagine the lights amplifying and sparkling signaling Archangel Metatron is approaching. Breathe in this divine connection. Archangel Metatron asks, "What would you like to manifest?"

Answer from your heart. You don't have to speak this aloud. Just mentally share your response.

Imagine Archangel Metatron asking, "Would you like my assistance?"

If you answer yes, then notice any intuitive insights. Trust the messages flowing to you through each of your five senses and your feelings and knowing.

Imagine your dream has manifested. Lean into that completion, experiencing the joy and gratitude.

With every inhale imagine energy flowing in, beginning below the souls of your feet up through out the top of your head. This vibrant, loving energy swirling through and around your body.

With every exhale, imagine all energetic blockages releasing and disintegrating.

When the timer sounds, thank Archangel Metatron. Take a cleansing breath and open your eyes.

You may want to sip on water afterward.

Journal any thoughts, visions, impressions you experience during the meditation. If journaling daily, ask Archangel Metatron and angels for additional insight. Thank them for their guidance.

If possible, do this exercise each day of the portal. If you can only do once then make sure you do this on 12/12.

Amplify the energy by performing this at at 12:12 am or pm or both.

"I am a divine manifesting magnet."

Retrogrades

Planets aren't really going backward. *Retrograde* is when it appears Earth has moved ahead of the planet, making the planet appears as if it's going backward.

Consider the root word, "retro," meaning "backward," and you have the energy for this phase. Retrograde is referring to the planets seeming motion of going backward, but this is a perfect manifesting time for going back in time.

- Revisit times you succeeded.
- Remember your dreams.
- Reminisce about things you did that kept your energy up.

This is a time to explore the "re's." Recycle. Reinforce. Reflect. Retrospective. Go backward in time and contemplate how you can glean knowledge from your prior experiences. How can you use that lesson or wisdom to help you manifest today?

Each planet lends its areas of expertise. When the planet is retrograding, these fields of expertise are the best for exploring memory lane to reveal its manifesting intel. For example, one of Mercury's areas of expertise is communication. When retrograding, think of a time you manifested something. What were you saying to yourself, to others and to the universe? Remembering these affirmations will reconnect you with a successful time. You'll know how to repeat this success and look at this manifesting cycle with a fresh approach.

Manifesting with each retrograde and its planet is included in the planet chapter.

2022 Retrograde Schedule by Month

JANUARY
Uranus Retrograde until 18 January
Venus Retrograde until 29 January
Mercury Retrograde 14 January – 3 February

FEBRUARY
Mercury Retrograde until 3 February

MARCH
No Retrogrades

APRIL
Pluto Retrograde 29 April – 8 October

MAY
Pluto Retrograde – 8 October
Mercury Retrograde 10 May – 3 June

JUNE
Pluto Retrograde – 8 October
Mercury Retrograde until 3 June
Saturn Retrograde 4 June – 23 October
Neptune Retrograde 28 June – 3 December

JULY

Pluto Retrograde – 8 October

Saturn Retrograde – 23 October

Neptune Retrograde – 3 December

Chiron Retrograde 19 July – 23 December

Jupiter Retrograde 28 July – 23 November

AUGUST

Pluto Retrograde – 8 October

Saturn Retrograde – 23 October

Neptune Retrograde– 3 December

Chiron Retrograde – 23 December

Jupiter Retrograde – 23 November

Uranus Retrograde 24 August – 22 January 2023

SEPTEMBER

Pluto Retrograde – 8 October

Saturn Retrograde – 23 October

Neptune Retrograde – 3 December

Chiron Retrograde – 23 December

Jupiter Retrograde – 23 November

Uranus Retrograde – 22 January 2023

Mercury Retrograde 9 September – 2 October

OCTOBER

Pluto Retrograde until 8 October

Saturn Retrograde until 23 October

Neptune Retrograde – 3 December

Chiron Retrograde – 23 December

Jupiter Retrograde – 23 November

Uranus Retrograde – 22 January 2023

Mercury Retrograde until 2 October

Mars Retrograde 30 October – 12 January 2023

NOVEMBER

Neptune Retrograde – 3 December
Chiron Retrograde – 23 December
Jupiter Retrograde until 23 November
Uranus Retrograde – 22 January 2023
Mars Retrograde – 12 January 2023

DECEMBER

Neptune Retrograde – 3 December
Chiron Retrograde – 23 December
Uranus Retrograde – 22 January 2023
Mars Retrograde – 12 January 2023
Mercury Retrogade 29 December – 18 January 2023

Manifesting
with the
Planets

★

Each planet brings specific energy, focus and message. Whether the planet is your ruling planet or stationed direct or retrograde, the planet is offering unique guidance for your manifesting endeavors.

Meanings & Their Path

Planets are like our super cool successful and older relatives. They've seen things. They've experienced things. They KNOW things. This chapter is like sitting down and getting reacquainted with these family members. Each has their own quirks, specialties and brilliant advice. When we open to their guidance, they'll show us quicker manifesting paths.

All nine planets, (yes, nine. Pluto is still family), will be covered in this chapter. AND! You don't have to be an astrologer to understand the planets. Just from this section, you'll be able to understand how they naturally influence you and determine what aspects you can utilize for your manifesting needs.

A planet's movement is good to know and is marked in the monthly manifesting pages.

- *Direct* is when the planet is moving and grooving on its normal path in front of Earth. *Direct* is a manifesting time of forward momentum. Take action. This is when the planet is offering to hold our hands and guide us. Weeee!

- *Retrograde* is when the planet seems to be going backward from our point of view on Earth. *Retrograde* is a time of slowing down. Breathe. Remember your awesomeness from the past. Revisit and review our past in their areas of the planet's expertise -- and apply to our current manifesting needs. You don't have to remember this. This is spelled out for you each month.

- *Pre-shadow* (leading up to the change in direction from direct to retrograde) and *post-shadow* days (days following exiting the retrograde phase). While both periods showcase the energy, pre-shadow is the retrograde energy increasing and post-shadow is the retrograde energy decreasing.

Connect With Your Planet

When the planet is ruling your astrological sign, there is a deeper connection. It's as if you are the planet's favorite! They go out of their way to connect with you. Intuitively you'll sense the communication. It won't be loud, in fact, it'll be very subtle. I promise I'm not adding to your day's overflowing to-do list. I am asking you just be open to the sensations you experience, pause and ask your sixth sense for any clarification. "What is my planet telling me?"

Sounds weird. I know. But, as a Gemini, ruled by Mercury, he has helped me meet deadlines, speak the right messages, and have a heads up about traveling. He's had my back! Your planet will too!

When connecting with a planet, whether yours or not, there are some simple ways to energetically connect.

1. Listen to the sound of the planet. There are recordings of the sounds from outer space. You can find this on YouTube or on my YouTube playlist entitled, "Planets." Venus is one of my favorites!

2. Connect with the color of your ruling planet. Find or make a candle in the planet's color.

Sun – orange | Leo

Moon – black and white | Cancer

Mercury – gray | Gemini and Virgo

Venus – gray-blue | Taurus and Libra

Mars – reddish-brown | Aries and Scorpio

Jupiter – orange-white | Sagittarius and Pisces

Saturn – pale gold | Capricorn and Aquarius

Uranus – aquamarine | Aquarius

Neptune – dark blue | Pisces

Pluto – brown and cream | Scorpio

State your intention, *"I am connecting with the planet* _____ *(fill in the blank)."* Light your candle. Take a cleansing breath. Feel the connection. Keep your candle lit as long as you'd like. Before you extinguish the flame, thank the planet. This gratitude is a vibration and is felt by the universe.

3. Dedicate a crystal to be your planet's connection. This is *your* choice. You may intuitively feel a tektite, meteorite, or some crystal that seems an unusual option. Trust your intuition. Opals were discovered on Mars by the Mars Rover, so choose the crystal that you feel it is your link to your planet.

   Once you've chosen your crystal, hold it in both hands. Close your eyes and feel yourself opening to a deeper connection with the crystal and its tie to your planet. When you feel a bond has been created, thank the crystal and open your eyes. Slip the crystal in your pocket, place it in your sacred space or by your bed. You can choose to include the crystal in meditations or just connect while sleeping.

Now, time for the family reunion with the planets!

Sun

———

Sun, friendly, loving and original head of the family.
He loves you and fuels your manifesting fires.

QUIRKS: Sun is like the radiant, loyal, devoted dad of the family tree.

SPECIALTIES: Optimism. Vitality. Encouraging. Success.

FAVORITE SIGN: Leo

ADVICE: "Shine your unique light and manifest."

The sun is the divine masculine energy. He cheers you on. He knows you are equipped and able. The sun provides the fiery energy, fuels your confidence and the focus to manifest.

Your sun sign attributes are the strengths and the chinks in your personality. This driving force sets us up to manifest – success or failure. So every time you look at the sun, remember to keep your focus on manifesting the outcome you desire. Just like the sunflower growing into a vibrant display of beauty, it starts with a seed. And, so does manifesting. Plant your seed in the fertile ground of your soul. Nurture with your intentional thoughts and mindset. And allow the sun to shine on your dreams.

The sun reminds you to celebrate you. Your personality and its strengths are part of your divine purpose. Your gifts stem from your awareness of your beautiful personality and the part it plays in your manifesting.

One of my favorite Aesop Fables is The North Wind and the Sun. They're having a chat regarding who's stronger and spot a man in a coat along the road. A deal is struck that whoever gets the man to remove his coat is declared the stronger. The wind blows and blows, of course, the man clenches his coat tighter. The sun shines and shines, and the man eagerly removes his coat.

Manifesting with the sun is like that. No need to force. Stay positive. Shine and allow.

Work with the Sun when you want:

- Growth
- Abundance
- Focus
- Energy
- Confidence
- Acceptance
- Creativity

Sunshine for Manifesting

- Identify the sun's current sign and the qualities it offers. Apply the beneficial attributes to your manifesting plan.

- Get outdoors. Get in the sunshine. Soak up the Vitamin D and all the benefits. Imagine the sun warming your dreams and the fertile manifesting ground.

- Every time you look at the sun, remember to keep your focus on manifesting the outcome you desire. Just like the sunflower growing into a vibrant display of beauty, it starts with a seed. And, so does manifesting. Plant your seed in the fertile ground of your soul. Nurture with your intentional thoughts and mindset. And allow the sun to shine on your dreams.

Moon

___

Moon, inspiring, loving and compassionate ancient family.
She loves you and nurtures your soul, your dreams and deepest desires.

QUIRKS: Moon is like the quiet, nurturing and understanding,
devoted mom of the family tree.

SPECIALTIES: Emotions. Nurturing. Intuitive. Cycles.

FAVORITE SIGN: Cancer

ADVICE: "Align your emotions. Trust your intuition.
And, accept the fact that you are a divine magical being
already aligned with the manifesting flow."

The moon is the divine feminine energy. She goes deep. She reaches out to you every night. She knows by nurturing your soul and cocooning yourself in love, you emotionally open to receiving the bounty life has to offer. Whatever the deepest desires you truly want to manifest, the Moon wants to assist.

Moon communicates through emotions and intuition. How you're feeling and responding is telling you if you're truly aligned with receiving what you want to manifest or if you've got some blockages. Your intuition is the right path to manifest. Tune her out, and you risk incurring manifesting delays.

Work with Moon when you want to manifest in the areas of:

- Family and home
- Healing and understanding
- Spiritual work
- Fertility
- Aligning emotions with manifesting

The moon is associated with goddesses throughout time and cultures. She represents the phases of our life. She brings light, inspiration and love. Wherever you are in your manifesting cycle, the moon will embrace, encourage, and empower you. Explore the moon chapter for deepening your moon connection.

Mercury

———

*Mercury, chatty and sometimes obnoxious, is still your
wise, albeit, snarky ancient nephew. He loves you and will
give your manifesting dreams wings to take flight.*

QUIRKS: Mercury is the excited, energetic and chatty nephew.

SPECIALTIES: Communication. Contracts. Travel. Electronics.

FAVORITE SIGNS: Gemini and Virgo

ADVICE: "Clear up your affirmations and you'll clear your
path to speedy manifesting of your dreams."

Mercury is closest to the Sun. He zips around, cheering us on and inspiring action. Mercury provides the extra energy and warmth when we hit a wall, need clarity or creative inspiration.

Work with Mercury when you want:

Knowledge about going forward. For example, if you want to manifest a new car, Mercury guides you to the vehicle pros and cons and even will reveal a better deal.

Communication — hearing and sharing your intuition, communicating with others, communicating with angels or spirit guides, speaking, writing, and networking.

- Create your affirmations for manifesting
- Communicate your dreams with others
- Reconnect with youthful energy and belief

When Mercury is Retrograde

It can seem like Mercury is always retrograding. That's because he does three to four times a year. Given the not-so-loving nickname, "The Trickster," when retrograde, Mercury messes up our phones, computers, cars, travel plans and creates this intense desire to hook back up with an ex.

Mercury Retrograde doesn't have to be a bad time.

Navigate Mercury Retrograde:

- Give yourself extra time with any appointments or necessary travel
- Review texts, emails and calendar days and times
- Think. And think again before you speak

Mercury Retrograde for Manifesting

Remember a time from the past when your dream came true. Think back and reminisce of what you thought and said. Reconnect to the excitement and gratitude of the successful journey, even the bumps encountered along the way.

Don't get frustrated when any glitches occur. Immediately explore if a new door is opening. Perhaps a door that had been opened in the past and since forgotten.

This retrograde may bring just the one to help you manifest what you want!

Gemini and Virgo, you'll be impacted more than other signs. Mercury Retrograde will lend its curiosity to explore more of the out-of-the-box thinking and dreams. You'll also be able to see the pros and cons of man-ifesting your dream. Use this time to talk yourself into pursuing your dreams.

Venus

————

*Venus, elegant and feminine, is your nurturing, albeit, sexy
ancient auntie. She loves you and will provide your manifesting
with the love and kindness it needs to succeed.*

QUIRKS: Venus is the gorgeous, confident and elegant auntie.

SPECIALTIES: Beauty, Arts. Money. Love.

FAVORITE SIGNS: Taurus and Libra

ADVICE: "Embrace love in all things and you will be
a magnet for manifesting your dreams."

Venus is often seen in our sky and felt in our hearts. She calls out to us in the allure of a song, elegance in art, and the magnificence of mother nature. She encourages us to celebrate our own unique gifts and beauty. Venus provides the extra confidence when we're ready to take a risk, put our hearts out there or need to love and accept ourselves again.

Work with Venus when you want:

To attract beauty, wealth and love. For example, if you want to manifest a better relationship, Venus guides you to the steps to take beginning with loving yourself. By doing this, you're communicating to the universe that you are worthy, deserving and ready to receive what you want to manifest.

Cooperation — getting support from those around, including your boss and co-workers, family members, and friends.

- Create your vision board for manifesting
- Decorate your bedroom, sacred space, home or office
- Dream and align with your dream having already come true
- Open the energy of balance and harmony in your life
- Reconnect with your soul's passion
- Reveal your soul's passion

When Venus is Retrograde

Venus can throw our love life and finances into havoc. Harmony on the home front may be challenged. Ex-lovers may try to connect. Credit cards and online banking may go on the fritz. This is the time to sit and be beautiful.

Venus Retrograde is always offering love and support.

Navigate Venus Retrograde

- Do NOT try a new haircut, makeup regimen or major beauty shift
- Do make extra time for delving into self-care and self-love
- Splurge on enjoying the luxury already in your life

Venus Retrograde for Manifesting

Remember a time when you felt prosperous or really loved. Go all in exploring this memory lane. Connect with every emotion. Recall the joy, appreciation and magic through each of your senses. To anchor this energy, draw an abstract that captures the beauty, love and gratitude.

This retrograde may bring just the one to help you manifest what you want!

Taurus and Libra you'll be impacted more than other signs. Venus Retrograde will lovingly show you where you may be out-of-balance. She'll ask you to remember you are worthy and deserving of love and your dreams.

Mars

———

Mars, courageous and sometimes arrogant, is still your strong, assertive ancient cousin. He loves you and will push your dream from beginning to champion status.

QUIRKS: Mars is like the confident, get-it-done, jock cousin.

SPECIALTIES: Strength. Courage. Competitive. Physical.

FAVORITE SIGNS: Aries and Scorpio

ADVICE: "Take action! Do one thing each day and you will be on the victorious side of manifesting your dreams."

Mars is like the athletic young jock whose energy is contagious. He knows how to win and sweeps you into the enthusiastic confidence. Mars provides the tenacity to help you get up when feeling discouraged, have the determination to pursue a new dream or the intestinal fortitude during any opposition.

Work with Mars when you want:

Fearlessness to pursue your dreams. Energy, courage and confidence to overcome any obstacle. Training necessary to achieve our goal.

- Create a plan of action to manifest your dreams
- Put blinders on and listen to the confidence and encouragement of your soul
- Reconnect with inner and outer strength

When Mars is Retrograde

Forget arguing about what's fair and what isn't. Sex may seem off. Things can seem all stumbling into a brick wall. This is a perfect time to go within. Where are you doubting yourself? What are you truly communicating to yourself? Do you honestly know you are a winner? Deserving? If not, this retrograde is the perfect time to sniff out the blockages and open to your strengths. Exit this retrograde knowing you are a champion!

Navigate Mars Retrograde

- Explore new workout programs
- Look in the mirror and give yourself pep talks
- Avoid arguments

Mars Retrograde for Manifesting

Get moving! Go for a walk, run, or stretch. While you are moving, state your affirmations out loud. *"I am confident in pursuing and achieving my dreams! I have manifested my dreams!"* You are calling in the dream manifested as you are taking the steps. Your whole mind, body and spirit is engaged.

This can be a time of interference and glitches. People may be cranky or increasingly negative about your dreams. Do not give any energy to entertaining those distractions. Stay focused. Concentrate on your win.

This retrograde may bring just the one to help you manifest what you want!

Aries and Scorpio, you'll be impacted more than other signs. Mars Retrograde will lends its power to discovering beneficial detours and new action steps. You'll also be able to see where you have succeeded before and the knowingness that you will succeed again! Use this time to pump yourself up and know you are achieving your dreams.

Jupiter

—

*Jupiter, big, bold, and sometimes honest to a fault is still a
kind and helpful ancient uncle. He loves you and will reward
your faith and optimism that dreams do come true.*

QUIRKS: Jupiter is like the friendly, enthusiastic and rich uncle.

SPECIALTIES: Adventure. Good Luck. Opportunities. Electronics.

FAVORITE SIGNS: Sagittarius and Pisces

ADVICE: "Be open to the generosity of the universe.
Once you do, prosperity showers upon you!"

*O*ften identified as the "Daddy Warbucks" of the planets, Jupiter offers his wallet open to you. What do you need? I'm gonna help! Jupiter doesn't just give the financial assist. It's the good luck, new ideas, and opportunities. Jupiter has the attitude and belief that 'of course the dream has manifested!'

Work with Jupiter when you want:

To manifest! Jupiter knows how to find the shower of blessings.

Need to take a risk. Jupiter will help you shine and thrive.

Working with Jupiter leads to expansion and growth within your life – spiritually, mentally and physically. You'll boldly find yourself changed for the better.

- Fearlessness to seize the moment, opportunity and good fortune
- Explore new areas of wisdom to achieve your dreams
- Be open to new and easier ways of receiving good luck

When Jupiter is Retrograde

Overdoing it? Places of excess? Areas where you focus on the half-empty. This teaching and wise planet will lovingly reveal places where change must occur.

Navigate Jupiter Retrograde

- Set better and clearer boundaries
- Trust your inner knowingness for the answers
- Let go of the things, thoughts, and beliefs that restrict your joy, love, and success

Jupiter Retrograde for Manifesting

Go all out on positive affirmations. Splurge! Jupiter has the insider knowledge to the right path to manifest easier and faster. So focus your energy and attention on this.

Practice daily gratitude. Maybe you're already writing in a gratitude journal, but if you'll increase your gratitude, you will increase your manifesting magnetism.

This retrograde may bring just the one to help you manifest what you want!

Sagittarius and Pisces you'll be impacted more than other signs. Jupiter Retrograde will lends its loving approach to search your self-expression. By being generous, you receive generosity. By being kind, you receive kindness. By being loving, you receive love. This retrograde offers a chance to boost your vibration and align with higher frequencies of love and abundance.

Saturn

——

Saturn, strict, serious and rather old-school-rigid-teacher, is still your brilliant and mature ancient uncle. He loves you and will provide the plan, steps and priorities and if you'll do the work you'll find your dreams manifested easier and faster.

QUIRKS: Saturn is like the strict, no fun and boring uncle.

SPECIALTIES: Commitment. Structure. Rules. Teacher.

FAVORITE SIGNS: Capricorn and Aquarius

ADVICE: "Use your time wisely and you'll manifest your dreams."

℠ aturn use to be considered the edge of the universe. He embodied the phrase, "the buck stops here," meaning he was the gatekeeper, the ruler and enforcer of hard work. No skimping. Just do it.

Work with Saturn when you want:

Structure. Whether building a home, writing a book or laying out ingredients for a recipe, structure makes the process easier. That's what Saturn reveals. The best structure for the best end result.

- Take responsibility for your dreams manifesting

- Overcoming procrastination
- Prioritizing and scheduling so your life has balance and dreams have room to come true

When Saturn is Retrograde

He's reminding you that you matter. Your opinions, beliefs and goals matter. Stay realistic. Do not set yourself up for failure. Retrograde will help you see where you are trying to squeeze thirty hours of work into a twenty-four hour day. Use this time to strike a sensible and healthy balance.

Navigate Saturn Retrograde

- Identify areas needing closure and shut that door so you can open to the success
- Take an honest look at where you seem blocked from progress and make the necessary changes
- Make a list of priorities, put blinders on and set timers to complete your list

Saturn Retrograde for Manifesting

Is there a mentor who has achieved what you want? Whether you know this person or not, look to see the system they had in place. What steps did they take? What boundaries, schedules, disciplines did they use? Create a framework that will work for you. No rush. Do the research. Do the work. Create your personalized design. Saturn will reward your hard work when he goes direct.

This retrograde may bring just the one to help you manifest what you want!

Capricorn and Aquarius, you'll be impacted more than other signs. Saturn Retrograde will provide a realistic view of your energy and where you're giving it. Are you giving too much to others and it's taking away energy and focus from your dreams? Set clear and realistic boundaries. Remember, every time you say "yes" to someone else, you are saying "no" to you. Trust the process. Stay balanced and know that you are worthy of wonderful opportunities.

Uranus

_____

Uranus, cool, unconventional and sometimes peculiar, is still
your brilliant ancient uncle. He loves you and will provide
a radical, fresh, genius new take on manifesting.

QUIRKS: Uranus is like the innovative, eccentric and rebellious uncle.

SPECIALTIES: Technology. Inventions, Rational Thinking, Electronics

FAVORITE SIGNS: Aquarius

ADVICE: "Expect the unexpected and you'll discover manifesting
your dreams in ways you didn't know possible."

U ranus is unique, original and extremely comfortable in his own way
of doing things. He is the only planet that spins horizontally rather
than vertically. I always envisioned Uranus as the Steve Jobs, co-found-
er of Apple, of the solar system. He brings sudden change with his new
ideas and technological advances.

Work with Uranus when you want:

A new, radical approach for an area in your life. Maybe it's time to shake
things up. Branch out into the unknown. Maybe it's time to escape into
deeper meditation or exploring new elements of your spirituality.

- Being comfortable being uniquely you
- Logic and reasoning to be the guiding force
- Major modifications in your life

When Uranus is Retrograde

Uranus shakes things up creating turmoil and sudden change. As you're sorting through the aftermath, Uranus seems to be saying, "Here you go. Deal with it. You're welcome." It can seem like a pile of chaos, but when the topsy-turviness settles, you'll discover a hidden gem.

Uranus Retrograde doesn't have to be rife with disappointments.

Navigate Uranus Retrograde

- Discover areas of your life that need some liberating or transformation
- Explore online courses, lectures, and new audiobooks
- Celebrate your own quirks, preferences, and unique personality

Uranus Retrograde for Manifesting

Are there areas in your life needing fresh energy and new ideas? Maybe you've become too logical and are thinking, *"It has to manifest this way."* Uranus Retrograde is the perfect time to recall a time you've gone out of your comfort zone and succeeded. Invite discomfort in and let the success begin!

Uranus Retrograding is an opportune time to try that new way of doing something. Get out of the rut and explore. Uranus really does bring breakthroughs in areas that have been stymied. Retrograde will help you see what areas of your life need a shakeup and the new ways to achieve this.

This retrograde may bring just the one to help you manifest what you want!

Aquarius, you'll be impacted more than any other sign. Uranus Retrograde will have you reaching out to heal the world. You'll see where your dreams will make the world a better place. By investing in spiritual endeavors like meditation, yoga or other creating healing mandalas you'll receive new insight into manifesting your dreams.

Neptune

———

*Neptune, mystical and magical, is still your transforming
ancient uncle. He loves you and will empower your
spiritual gifts so you can make manifesting magic.*

QUIRKS: Neptune is like the handsome, mysterious and romantic uncle.

SPECIALTIES: Imagination. Dreams. Spiritualism. Compassion.

FAVORITE SIGNS: Pisces

ADVICE: "Go deep into your divine self. Accept your creative and magical
powers and you will flow in the ever-present manifesting current."

N eptune known as "God of the Sea" swims besides you as you plunge
into the deep waters of your soul. He carries a triton that looks like
a tuning fork, enabling you to tune into your dreams and the smooth-
est way to manifest them. Look for his influence and encouragement
through music!

Work with Neptune when you want:

Inspiration! Maybe you long for your muse to whisper, encourage, and
arouse the passion within. Neptune aligns with change in your life with-

out extreme waves. Neptune ushers in shifts with ease and subtly. This includes healing, artistic expression and nurturing your soul.

- Deepen your spiritual gifts, especially intuition and sensitivities to the spirit world
- Increase compassion in your life with others and yourself
- Ease in expressing yourself

When Neptune is Retrograde

It's a time to go deeper and move beyond any illusions. Where are you kidding yourself? You'll be able to identify and see the realities of situations and relationships. You'll also be able to see where you're romanticizing and ignoring the reality of a situation. Neptune Retrograde will show you where you are sacrificing yourself and it's taking a toll on you physically, spiritually, and mentally. Once he's ripped off the rose-colored glasses you'll be able to make swift changes so you can swim in the deep manifesting waters.

Navigate Neptune Retrograde

- Open to releasing the old and welcoming in the new in a smooth, fluid
- Schedule in spa days, self-care and spiritual retreats
- Keep a dream journal

Neptune Retrograde for Manifesting

What spiritual or new age topic have you wanted to explore? This is the time to fully engage. Pay attention to your intuition as you seek answers through your spiritual pursuits. Maybe you suddenly want to explore becoming a Reiki Master or investing in working with crystals. Divine guidance will be provided. Be open to the known and unknown. Trust your sixth sense!

This retrograde may bring just the one to help you manifest what you want!

Pisces, you'll be impacted more than any other sign. Neptune Retrograde will offer clarity as to who you are and why your dreams matter. You'll gain confidence as this timing rips the bandages off and reveals where you may be stuck. You'll identify the situations, people or even your thoughts that have been holding you back from achieving your success. In Retrograde, the murky fog is lifted. The path is cleared. You will be able to see and know what to do to confidently manifest your dreams.

Pluto

---

*Pluto, mysterious and intense, is still your powerful ancient
cousin. He loves you and will assist in taking your dreams
from the caterpillar to the butterfly manifesting stage.*

QUIRKS: Pluto is like the quiet, intense and goth cousin.

SPECIALTIES: Secrets. Death. Rebirth. Power. Control.

FAVORITE SIGNS: Scorpio

ADVICE: "Even when people tell you that you can't
or that you're nothing... use this opportunity to
reach deep within and prove them wrong."

P luto is a small and mighty planet. He is wonderful helping in manifesting. He'll hold your hand in his and escort you to the depths of
your soul. He'll shine light into the areas needing a swift demise. Once
accomplished, Pluto gives you the fiery energy and tenacious confidence
to rise like the phoenix. Working with Pluto, you will soar higher than
ever before.

Work with Pluto when you want:

Secret talents revealed. Sometimes you take your gifts for granted. Sometimes you assume your talents are no good. Pluto helps you see that just is not so. Your hidden gifts are begging to come to light. Pluto will help this transformation.

- Set your inner most dreams free
- Release limiting beliefs, habits and hurts and rise like the Phoenix
- Intense and significant change with shadow work

When Pluto is Retrograde

Sometimes you're in a funk. It happens. Pluto Retrograde transforms you. No more wallowing or stuck in the pits. Pluto pulls you out of any pits blocking your manifesting! This covers every area: spiritually, physically, and emotionally.

Navigate Pluto Retrograde

- Explore shadow work (the darker areas of our personality/soul) with the intention of releasing and transforming
- Use this time for honest evaluation in every area of your life to see what you can, or should, release
- Examine areas of control. Are you allowing the magic to flow or exerting control and wanting to manifest your way instead?

Pluto Retrograde for Manifesting

And the truth shall set you free. Pluto retrograde provides the spotlight on the areas causing any manifesting limitations. Whether from a past life or current programing, this is the time to shine the light on the inner constraints. Obliterate the emotional chains of fear, insecurities and doubt. Be open to the confidence and spiritual guidance and accept your inner power. Pluto retrograde will eradicate the obstacles so you can tune into being the manifesting superstar you were created to be.

This retrograde may bring just the one to help you manifest what you want!

Scorpio you'll be impacted more than other signs. Pluto Retrograde will reveal your inner secrets -- even the ones you've been keeping from yourself. Apply this energy to shed what's not working and embrace and reclaim your passion and power!

Chiron

———

Chiron, friendly, loving and compassionate ancient family.
He loves you and frees you to manifest your dreams deepest desires.

QUIRKS: Chiron is like the sensitive, kind, maverick in the family tree.

SPECIALTIES: Healing. Teacher. Abandonment. Compassion.

FAVORITE SIGNS: He doesn't play favorites to ensure no one is left out.

ADVICE: "Heal yourself. Step into your unique greatness and
then you'll be victorious in manifesting your dreams."

C hiron is called a minor planet, comet, and an asteroid. His Greek story tells of abandonment, betrayal and rejection. A centaur (half-man, half-horse), Chiron constantly lived a unique path thanks to the upbringing of his adopted dad, Apollo. Unlike other centaurs who were very much bullies on the scene, Chiron was a healer, teacher, prophet, and supporter of the arts. He did not fit in. He teaches that you don't need to either. Celebrate your uniqueness. Celebrate your calling and your spiritual gifts.

Work with Chiron when you want:

Healing in any area of your life. Chiron knows the challenges of life. He knows rejection. He knows the path to healing and overcoming adversity, whether intentional or accidental. Chiron helps make lemonade out of life's lemons.

- Create healing and empowering affirmations
- Explore alternative healing
- Write inspirational and powerful poetry, memoirs and messages

When Chiron is Retrograde

Everyone has deep wounds. Chiron Retrograding is a time to identify and free yourself from any guilt. He helps you see the benefits of this hardship, so you truly walk away feeling stronger and worthy of success.

Navigate Chiron Retrograde

- Celebrate your uniqueness
- Release the hurt, pain, and deep-down rejection once and for all
- Indulge in self-care and schedule daily spoiling

Chiron Retrograde for Manifesting

No faking. No more lying to yourself. Why aren't you manifesting? What is at the core? Lean into this and identify each nook and cranny. Don't rush. Let this be revealed so you can address, release and overcome. Knowing that golden nugget that's been hampering your joy, your success, your dreams will topple over the rest of the blockages. Then write out, pen to paper, why you are worthy of manifesting this dream. Chiron will take this message to the heavens and shout it to the universe!

This retrograde may bring just the one to help you manifest what you want!

All signs are impacted. Chiron Retrograde is here to help. Use the gift of this magical, powerful healing time.

Manifesting
with the
Astrological Signs

Each sign brings specific energy, strengths and influences. Every sign brings specific energy for everyone to use. The signs are especially impactful when they are in your sun or moon.

Meanings & Manifesting

Astrology signs offer massive insight and manifesting energies. The signs are influential in your personal signs, moon cycles, and monthly positions.

Working with the astrological attributes provides a manifesting advantage. You're aligning with their cosmic forte and powerful flow.

This chapter covers the signs, along with their significance, so you can determine how you want to weave them in, borrow insight, and extract guidance to apply to your own manifesting.

When reviewing each signs properties....

- Note the active dates of the sign so you know the current manifesting energies.
- Pay attention to the ruling planet and explore the planet's strengths in the planet section.
- Explore the sign's strengths.
- Determine how you'd like to apply the sign's energy.
- Create your plan.

When the sun is in your ruling astrological sign, there is a deeper connection. It's as if the manifesting energies give you preferential attention.

Of course, no one has "favorites," but yes, they do. Seriously... utilize it.

If you don't know your astrological sign, you can search online for "natal birth chart" and enter your date, time, and location of your birth. There are many sites online that will give you your correct astrological sign. This is especially important if you were born on the "cusp" or during the transition from one astrological sign to another.

Aries

DATES: 20 March 11:33 am EDT – 18 April

SPECIALTIES: Energetic. Confident. Natural Leader. Entrepreneur.

FAVORITE PLANET: Mars

MOTTO: I am going to manifest it!

The first sign of the zodiac, Aries comes right out with manifesting power. Mindset and energy are aligned with making their dreams happen. Aries is a wonderful energy for manifesting anything and everything. They have the stamina, focus, and optimistic attitude to accomplish what they want.

ARIES MANIFESTING STRENGTHS

- Creating new business, career, opportunities
- Taking action on unfinished projects, and shelved manifesting dreams
- Overcoming a financial challenge
- Pursuing any solo endeavor or dream
- Making decisions

TO MANIFEST WITH THIS SIGN

- Know what you want.
- Write 5 ways you can take action to achieve this.
- Take action every day. Aries is all about action taking and accomplishment.
- Stay aligned with Aries

Taurus

DATES: 19 April 10:24 pm EDT – 19 May

SPECIALTIES: Loyal. Determined. Romantic.

FAVORITE PLANET: Venus

MOTTO: I am going to have it!

The determination of Taurus provides the tenacity and fortitude to manifest. This is perfect manifesting energy for attracting the finer things in life. Creative, strong and determined, Taurus will help you have the perfect plan and the energy to stay the course.

TAURUS MANIFESTING STRENGTHS

- Obtaining the finer things
- Increased creativity
- Energy and stubbornness to keep going
- Love and beauty

TO MANIFEST WITH THIS SIGN

Create a nice meal with all the scrumptiousness. This includes candles, pleasant music, nice plates, candles, linen napkins. Include a beautiful crystal or sentimental glass. This should feel extremely luxurious. Thoroughly enjoy this exquisite connection. As you're feeling appreciative of the moment, answer this: What would you want if money was no object? What would you truly want? If it's been awhile or you're so tuned out of your heart's desires, Taurus will help you remember the beautiful things, the loving relationship, and the joy of your exquisite soul. When you're tuning into the gifts of the Taurus energy, you're tuning into the talents of Leonardo da Vinci, Kelly Clarkson, and Dwayne Johnson who are all encouraging you to dream bigger!

Gemini

DATES: 20 May 9:22 pm EDT – 21 June

SPECIALTIES: Social. Curious. Spontaneous. Chatty.

FAVORITE PLANET: Mercury

MOTTO: I am going to talk it into manifesting!

Dazzling, chatty, zipping around Gemini will help you manifest without all the limitations of doing it "the right way." Playful Gemini helps your vibration remain high. The twins will help you have twice the manifesting energy if you'll let them!

GEMINI MANIFESTING STRENGTHS

- Being flexible
- Reaching out, exploring and networking new opportunities
- Ability to manifest several things at once
- Communicating the best manifesting thoughts and affirmations

TO MANIFEST WITH THIS SIGN

Communicate your manifesting desires. Know what you want. Script your thoughts and affirmations around that. Remember, Gemini is quick-minded. She's not going to linger on any affirmation. Neither will you! Write it down. Next!

Cancer

DATES: 21 June 5:13 am EDT – 21 July

SPECIALTIES: Emotional. Homebody. Super Psychic.

FAVORITE PLANET: Moon

MOTTO: I am going to nurture it into manifesting!

This water sign is ruled by the Moon! It's no wonder that this sign is a natural nurturer! Represented by the crab, Cancer's energy provides a wonderful opportunity to evaluate your boundaries!

CANCER MANIFESTING STRENGTHS

- Superhero intuition abilities...they just know that they know
- Nurturing through the calm and rough waters
- Home and family
- Successful small businesses and start-ups
- Knowing when you need to withdraw and nurture you

TO MANIFEST WITH THIS SIGN

Connect with Cancer energy in the shower, in the bath, or watching a water fountain. Look at the flow. This will be a time when your ideas are especially bountiful in the shower. Cancer has the natural abilities to go with the flow, step out, and hide within when needed and use their pincers to grasp and hold on.

Slipping a moonstone into your pocket creates a subtle connection to this sensitive sign. Keep carrying it until you've reached your goal. Even if the sun moves into other signs, Cancer will continue to support you until you've manifested this desire.

Leo

DATES: 22 July 4:06pm EDT – 21 August

SPECIALTIES: Bold. Courageous. Warmhearted.

FAVORITE PLANET: Sun

MOTTO: I am deserving of it being manifested!

Confident and Optimistic, Leo has the manifesting success spotlight. Popular, Leo is able to stand out in a crowd because of its gorgeous, presence and loyalty. Leos are exceedingly generous. Leo shares the manifesting spotlight.

LEO MANIFESTING STRENGTHS

- Courage to pursue dreams, even outlandish ones
- Playful and creative
- Stepping into your light
- Ambitious
- Able to excel and stand out in the crowd

TO MANIFEST WITH THIS SIGN

Imagine taking center stage. Lights are all on you. There is no fear... even if you have a history of stage fright. Leo is by you. Interviewing you. Sharing your success story with the world. In fact, Leo knows every juicy detail of your perseverance, your manifesting journey, and is singing your praises. Compliments are flowing.

Virgo

DATES: 22 August 11:16 pm EDT – 21 September

SPECIALTIES: Organized. Practical. Perfectionist. Helpful.

FAVORITE PLANET: Mercury

MOTTO: I've got a plan to manifest it!

Practical Virgo not only has a plan, she has a perfect, efficient plan. She can sort through a jumbled mess and connect the dots. Chaos doesn't belong in Virgo's world, so manifesting plans will be focused and simple to do. She'll also remind you of the importance of taking care of yourself so you can be healthy and enjoy your dreams manifested.

VIRGO MANIFESTING STRENGTHS

- Increased health and healing touch
- Exploring new skills
- Success whenever she puts her mind to it
- Implementing the right way

TO MANIFEST WITH THIS SIGN

Decide what you want to manifest and recruit Virgo's assistance. She'll create a plan and strategy to expertly achieve it. Preferring a system, Virgo ties in the manifesting steps perfectly.

1. Focused Intentional Thoughts.
2. Focused intentional actions.
3. Focused intentional manifesting.

Virgo will help you stay organized with your eyes on the prize.

Libra

DATES: 22 September 9:03pm EDT – 22 October

SPECIALTIES: Balanced. Diplomatic. Kind.

FAVORITE PLANET: Venus

MOTTO: There's plenty for all of us to manifest!

Libra wants a win for all. She's fair-minded, compromising and tactful. Charming Librans are able to gently turn any situation around because at the center of it all is… love. Like the famous Libran, Ghandi, this sign will peacefully reconnect everything with love. Love is that high vibration which makes for being a manifesting magnet.

LIBRA MANIFESTING STRENGTHS

- Creating a peaceful home, office, environment
- Calmness and adaptability
- Understanding a situation to help forgive and heal
- Believing it is possible
- Harmony

TO MANIFEST WITH THIS SIGN

Use the arts to connect with Libra. Grab a paint brush and canvas. Dance to classical music. Visit an art museum. Enjoy the joie de vivre as you connect with this Goddess Venus-ruled sign.

Manifest the love, beauty, and harmony into your life.

Scorpio

DATES: 23 October 6:35 am EDT – 21 November

SPECIALTIES: Passionate, Intuitive. Secretive.

FAVORITE PLANETS: Mars and Pluto

MOTTO: I demand it and it is manifested!

This water sign is mysterious, intimidating and magical. Ruled by Mars until Pluto stepped out of her shadow, Scorpio has a shroud of secrecy. And, Scorpio just *knows* things. Their intuitive inside tract is manifesting intensity. They set themselves up to succeed and will push it to the unknown to achieve it.

SCORPIO MANIFESTING STRENGTHS

- Intelligent and imaginative
- Know how to get what you want
- Transformation
- Self-control
- Stretching for the deep desires of our soul

TO MANIFEST WITH THIS SIGN

Explore working with a tarot deck or pendulum. Even if you've never picked either up, going into this deep territory brings psychic Scorpio along. Give yourself a reading and see the truth this honest sign delivers.

Sagittarius

DATES: 22 November 3:20 am EST – 20 December

SPECIALTIES: Adventurous. Inquisitive. Honest.

FAVORITE PLANET: Jupiter

MOTTO: Why do a subtle manifesting when you can go all the way?

This centaur brings the wild acceptance and thrill of your manifesting journey. Her optimism, openness, and excitement toward the possibilities allow to truly manifest "this or something better." She is a perpetual student and teacher so she's constantly learning new approaches to manifesting a wonderful life.

SAGITTARIUS MANIFESTING STRENGTHS

- Taking manifesting dreams to the next level
- Freedom and independence
- Humor
- Exploring new territory

TO MANIFEST WITH THIS SIGN

Explore new territory! This wanderlust sign brings the fun in discovering and learning. Travel outside and uncover new perspectives. Lie on the ground and look from a cat's point of view. Go horseback riding and look from the (almost) centaur's view. Or watch a documentary on the Andes. Explore the new with the curiosity and excitement of Sagittarius.

Capricorn

DATES: 21 December 4:48pm EST – 18 January

SPECIALTIES: Responsible. Hard working, Planner

FAVORITE PLANET: Saturn

MOTTO: Ain't no mountain high enough...
to keep me from manifesting what I want.

"If it ain't broke don't fix it," could be mumbled under Capricorn's breath. She's not going to waste time when there's a mountain to climb or a dream to achieve. There's a traditional way that works. Capricorn brings the "A" game, especially when needing laser focus to manifest one thing. You'll enjoy sharing the manifesting journey with this self-aware, natural leader.

CAPRICORN MANIFESTING STRENGTHS

- Extremely driven and extremely successful
- Manifesting for the long haul
- Able to remain focused until the dream is achieved
- Practical skills and clear goals for swift manifesting
- Detail-oriented and able to make quick adjustments

TO MANIFEST WITH THIS SIGN

Consider revisiting some of the original, everyday skills like sewing, carpentry, cooking, or gardening, skills that used to be the norm. These activities unlock memories and manifesting techniques. Capricorn doesn't mind the hard work and they expect the outcome they desire. Embrace your manifesting steps to make the most of this self-sufficient manifesting energy.

Aquarius

DATES: 19 January 9:39 pm EST – 17 February

SPECIALTIES: Intelligent. Quirky. Humanitarian.

FAVORITE PLANET: Uranus

MOTTO: Let's all manifest!

They love the crowd. Aquarius enjoys being a musketeer, all for one and one for all and please still give me my space. This dreamer is able to see the good that belongs to tomorrow. This is especially helpful when you're going through a difficulty, because Aquarius is able to provide hope.

AQUARIUS MANIFESTING STRENGTHS

- Incorporating technology
- Ideas that will benefit many
- Able to keep relaxed and confident about the outcome
- Scientific approach
- Detail-oriented and able to make quick adjustments

TO MANIFEST WITH THIS SIGN

This is a great time to manifest for the future. Starting a family, funds for retirement, or opening a rescue shelter, Aquarius will lend a helping hand. This is the time to implement the Cosmic Happenings for manifesting. This is right in Aquarius's wheelhouse. Pay attention to any online courses or connections Aquarius sends to you and stay open to the unexpected.

Pisces

DATES: 18 February 11:42 am EST – 19 March

SPECIALTIES: Intuitive. Artistic. Magical.

FAVORITE PLANET: Neptune and Jupiter

MOTTO: I go with the flow and I end up with
my dreams manifested! Let me help you!

The last sign of the zodiac, Pisces swims up and helps everyone. Wanting to provide assistance whether wanting to help you manifest health, money, or love, Pisces is there. It understands the ancient alchemy. It'll share alternative, creative, manifesting ideas. Compassionate and sensitive, Pisces is a natural empath. She believes in you and in your dreams. She'll do all she can to help... after her nap.

PISCES MANIFESTING STRENGTHS

- Exploring past lives to eliminate blockages
- Exploring past lives to remember success
- Able to find the best vibrational current
- Highly intuitive, they'll guide you to the perfect crystal or essential oil
- Able to take breaks and recharge (this really is a huge, beneficial strength)

TO MANIFEST WITH THIS SIGN

Record your own meditations. You can write your affirmations and record them or create your own full meditation. Then, rest. Snuggle. Doze. Pay attention to any intuitive dreams, for Pisces will continue to inspire you.

Manifesting
with the
Moon

The moon brings specific insight, discovery and guidance. Her energy is always accessible and empowering for every position of the manifesting cycle.

Manifesting is always possible. Manifesting with the moon energy makes the possible that much more possible.

Meanings & Manifesting Energies

The moon is powerful. She is constantly watching over us and we are connected. Just think of our emotions with the full moon, or how the moon impacts the tides, and how the moon cycle influences our crops.

We've been working with the moon and noting her importance for what it seems as long as there has been man. Ancient lunar calendars have been discovered around the world. Even then, there was an understanding of the importance of the moon, the cosmic cycles and the impact on the people.

We don't have to go to a cave to get the latest moon and cosmic cycles. The blessing of working with this energy still exists.

Working with the moon truly allows you to place yourself in the nurturing flow of success.

You'll learn how to navigate the moon's current cycle and how to use it to your manifesting advantage.

A little moon background. While a lady doesn't like to share her age, let's just say the beautiful goddess doesn't look a day over 4.53 billion years. She hangs out in our sky 238,000 miles away.

She rules over the astrological sign, Cancer, but offers her influence to all. The moon's specialties are connecting with your emotions, feminine energies, enhancing your intuition and spiritual gifts, exploring deeper introspection, receptivity and intimacy.

The moon is the divine feminine energy. She goes deep. She'll hold your hand, nurture your soul, and wrap you in love, enabling you to emotionally spread your wings and be open to receiving. Whatever the deepest desires you truly want to manifest, the Moon wants to assist. Our ancestors knew this!

Did you know that our ancestors from the Ice Age were carving lunar calendars 34,000 years ago?

Working with Cycles of the Moon

- *New Moon* is when the moon is not visible in the sky. This marks a fresh start. It is a time for planting new seeds of desires, setting new intentions, and conceiving new dreams that you want to manifest.

- *First Quarter* is when the moon looks half full. This is the time for going all in emotionally and physically. This is the time of laser focus and taking action toward manifesting.

- *Full Moon* is when the moon is totally full! You've come a long way, baby! You've put in the work. Celebrate all that has happened. Fill your soul with gratitude. Allow the full moon to illuminate any areas that can be tweaked. This is a great time to read your cards, ask angels for divine insight, and meditate on your dream already manifested.

- *Last Quarter* is when the moon is half full. Assess your progress. What changes are necessary. How can you modify under the next

New Moon cycle. Begin to release what is no longer supporting your manifesting desires.

- *Waxing* is the moon cycle from the New Moon to the Full Moon. Energy increases during this time. This is the time for building, increasing, and growth.

- *Waning* is the moon cycle from Full Moon to New Moon. Energy is diminishing. This is a time of releasing what isn't working and allowing it to be subtly released and pulled away.

- *Lunar Eclipse* is when the Earth's shadow is blocking the sun's light. The light is stopped. Lunar Eclipse is a time to go within, unlike a solar eclipse which impacts your physical body and taking action. This Lunar Eclipse is the time to get emotionally naked. The truth is there to be seen. What isn't serving you anymore? What emotional cycle is blocking your manifesting? Address and release for a swift and total emotional prosperous shift. *Eclipses deliver powerful and accelerated change.*

- *Supermoon* is when the moon is at its closest point to the Earth. During this time, the moon is 30% brighter and 14% larger. This occurs as a *Super New Moon* and a *Super Full Moon*. During these occasions the moon's manifesting aspects and energies are intensified.

Deepen Your Moon Connection

*C*onnecting with the moon fuels our divine feminine. This feeds our emotions and nurtures our soul. Here are some simple ways to energetically connect.

1. Sit outside under the night sky.

Find the perfect, comfortable spot. Sitting on a chair or a blanket, gaze into the sky and find the moon. Notice her current cycle and whether she's in the waxing or waning period. Both bring energy and clarity.

Take a cleansing breath as you ground your energy by connecting with earth below you. Take another cleansing breath as you imagine sending a stream of pink light from your heart all the way to the moon. Imagine her welcoming it and receiving it. Imagine she sends beams of love and connection back to you. Connect with this energy. When you feel like you are bathing in her light, take another cleansing breath. Thank her for her guidance and wisdom. Remember, even if you don't see her light, she is always in the sky.

2. Work with a crystal.

Any crystal will do. Moonstone, Opal, and Labradorite are my favorite for connecting with the powerful goddess energy. Goddess energy provides love, nurturing, strength, and the intuitive power to *know* how to manifest.

Choose the crystal that you intuitively feel you want to use for your moon connection. Hold it in both of your hands. As you're holding the crystal, close your eyes. Feel any energy in the crystal. When you're ready, ask the moon to imbue her energy into this crystal.

Perhaps you'll feel a warmth or tingles in your hands. Perhaps it will only be a knowing that the connection is there. Slip this crystal into your pocket. Every time you feel, touch, or see your crystal, know that you have this magical connection.

3. Bathe in the moonlight.

Find the area where moon is streaming in through your window or door. Snuggle into the light. As you feel the light shining on you, state affirmations or things you appreciate and love about yourself. Journal eight (eight is a magical manifesting number) things you're grateful for since you have manifested your dreams!

Give yourself an oracle reading in the moonlight.

The moon will provide the intuition and answers. By using an oracle deck to get a closer connection, you'll open the door to her manifesting energy and communication.

Take a cleansing breath while holding your deck between your palms. Ask for clarity on what you want to manifest. You can lay down one, three, or as many cards as you'd like. Trust your intuition with the divine message.

I like to do the one or three cards. The one card reading I feel is usually pretty straightforward. When I lay down the three cards, often, the first is my emotional blockage from the past, the second is the present message I need to hear, and the last is the advice to go forward.

Keep track of the message and symbols or images that stood out to you.

4. Make moon water.

Moon water is water imbued with the energy of the moon's cycle and the blessing each cycle brings.

Using a clean glass jar or other glass container, fill it with water. (I use distilled water, but any water is fine.) Put the glass outside in the moon's path and leave overnight. Bring the glass in the next morning. Label your jar so you know which cycle you captured. Store in a dark cabinet.

Use this water for amplifying the moon's manifesting energy.

- Dab it on your crystal, third eye, or throat chakra.
- Add it to your bath.
- Pour into your diffuser and add essential oils for an extra manifesting boost.

ESSENTIAL OIL BLENDS I LIKE:

- New Moon – Orange, Clary Sage, and Frankincense
- First Quarter – Peppermint, Grapefruit, and Lemon
- Full Moon – Ylang Ylang, Sandalwood, and Rose
- Last Quarter – Rosemary, Lemongrass, and Palo Santo

DISCLAIMER: *Always check with your doctor if you have any medical concerns, issues, or allergies. Always check the safety data before using any essential oils. Always use additional caution during pregnancy and with children and pets.*

Using the Moon Cycle for Manifesting

New Moon

This is the beginning of the manifesting cycle. You've done your part to make sure you have good manifesting soil (your mindset and emotions are aligned with receiving). This is the time to set new intentions of what you want to manifest. This always carries the energy of new.

Dates, astrological signs, and times for the new moon are included later. Manifesting suggestions for each specific new moon later in the Moon Cycles for 2022.

New moon topics for manifesting are focused on the new energies and fresh starts. This is superb for even reviving a stale relationship, seemingly dried-up opportunities, and new confidence or faith in manifesting.

To manifest with the new moon, write your New Moon Intention in a journal or someplace you will have access to throughout the moon cycle. *This is to be handwritten.* You want your connection and energy flowing into the seeds you want to prosper.

Hold your New Moon Intention in your hands and place against your heart. Offer gratitude for this manifested.

Say something like, *"These are my New Moon intentions. I promise to stay open to the divine guidance so this may manifest easier and faster. I know my desires have already come true. It is with much appreciation and gratitude, and with harm to none, that I receive this or something better lovingly manifested. Thank you."*

Put this New Moon Intention where you can easily access it and where the moon will shine through the window offering its growing light. Even if the moon isn't streaming through that window, the moon illuminates the sky and the light will touch your intention sheet.

I like placing mine in my sacred space. However, before I had a sacred space, I used my windowsill or on my nightstand next to my bed.

Super charge your New Moon Intention sheet by adding items that amplify the manifesting energy to your sheet.

- symbols of what you want manifested (like a heart for love, loose change for more wealth, a smiley face for joy)
- crystals
- chimes
- mirror
- glitter
- any items you intuitively feel

Crescent Moon

Within a day or two, the crescent moon begins lending her energy. This is easy to identify. You'll see the sliver of the moon that looks like a sideways Mona Lisa smile. This smile increases and is at its complete crescent phase within 7 days.

This is a time to commit to your intention. Gather wisdom from the cosmic energy being offered like the astrological sign and month's energy, write affirmations or light a candle.

When writing affirmations, remember to state in positive terms and as though it's already materialized.

Let's say you want to manifest money. Your affirmation could be, *"My income is constantly increasing."* Or *"I am prosperous."*

When adding a candle, be deliberate about your choice. Which intuitively feels like the right candle for your new moon intentions? Does size, shape or color matter? Do you want to make your own? Soy vs. Beeswax? Or does that not matter and you know the perfect candle?

Once your candle is chosen, hold the candle between both hands and bless it by saying,

"I bless you and thank you for sharing your manifesting energy."

At this point, you can place with your new moon intention sheet and this phase is concluded.

You can also go another step by lighting your candle.

If you choose to light your candle, set your candle on a safe, flat surface. (Upon your intention sheet if possible)

Light your candle and state, *"This light is special and will shine bright, blessing my dreams each and every night."*

Take a moment and imagine your dreams manifested. Visual how that looks and feels. Stay visualizing until you intuitively feel that you have connected with this manifestation. You may find a smile suddenly appearing on your face!

Blow out your candle and as the smoke swirls upward say, *"Thank you angels for manifesting this or something better."*

Leave the sheet and candle for the entire moon cycle.

Here are color meanings according to our ancient ancestors for your reference. Always trust your intuition when choosing.

- Yellow: wisdom, spirituality, sun
- Green: spring, rebirth, wealth
- Blue: improved health, clear skies, opportunities
- Orange: power, movement, endurance
- Red: passion, hope, love
- Brown: happiness, good harvest, healthy foundation
- Purple: faith, belief
- Pink: success
- Black: remembrance

First Quarter Moon

This is when the moon looks half-full. This is 7 – 10 days from the New Moon. This is the waxing period as the moon increases on its way to becoming full. The first quarter moon for every month is listed later within this section, as well as in the month-at-a-glance section.

This is a time to take action! Analyze what's working and what isn't and make any adjustments. Create additional action steps and release any tension with a good belly laugh. Manifesting is fun, not another job or task to be completed.

This is a perfect time to slip in some confidence-boosting techniques.

MIRROR WORK

Do this first thing in the morning and last thing at night and every time you pass a mirror. Look at yourself and declare that you are worthy. Choose from one of the following or create one of your own.

"I am deserving and worthy of my dreams."
"It is safe me to stand out and shine."
"I am a beautiful, priceless treasure."

CHOOSE YOUR THEME SONG

What type of song is your happy place? Quick tempo? Slow? Instrumental? Sing along?

Set your timer. No overthinking. Choose your theme song.

Once you've decided, give it a go and listen to your theme song.

Still loving it? Great! Now, strike a power pose in front of the mirror as your song plays. Hold this pose for as long as you're able. Let the pose and music blend into this powerful moment. Anytime you hear your theme song, remember to the world you are a super hero and the universe is picking you!

HERE ARE 2 POWER POSES

1. *Super Hero!* Feet grounded, hands on hip, chin up and chest out.

2. *Pick Me!* Feet planted on the ground, raise your arms straight up over your head (like the arm motion for the "Y" in the song "YMCA" by Village People) Turn your palms and face up to the sky. Smile.

Full Moon

The moon is seen completely round and easy to spot in the night sky.

This is the time to review your new moon intentions. See what modifications come to light. The full moon is the goddess energy. She has the higher view and is able to lovingly illuminate any hidden fears, forgotten steps, and areas needing adjustments. Trust this guidance. Take action and get back on track.

Each full moon is in an astrological sign which contributes a unique manifesting energy. Dates, sign and times are included later in this section and with manifesting suggestions in the month-at-a-glance section.

Here are two ways to connect with the full moon.

SELF-CARE HOUR

Just like the full moon is fully round, give yourself a full sixty minutes focused on you. This can be anything from reading your favorite romance novel to enjoying your favorite tv show. Make this deliberate and active.

Here are some other ideas.

- Get a manicure
- Make a smoothie
- Garden
- Snuggle with your pet

CREATE A MANDALA

Mandala literally means "circle" and is from the ancient Sanskrit language. Circles have been drawn forever in nature. When you draw your circle you're connecting with the energy of the universe, including the moon.

Grab your supplies (blank paper and pencils) and get comfortable.

- Visualize the full moon.
- Draw a circle on your paper.
- Visualize your intention manifested.

- Once you feel the joy of this manifested, begin drawing within your circle.
- This can be a scene, splashes of color, symbols, or even more circles. Trust your intuitive creativity. Go with the flow and draw.

No critiquing or judging your work. This is an intimate connection with the moon. Your mandala is coming out exactly as it's supposed to.

Draw until you feel complete. When finished, admire your work. See if there are any hidden images or messages within your art. Is there a color you're naturally drawn to. Even if nothing stands out, compliment yourself for this wonderful union with the moon and your dreams.

Put your mandala someplace safe.

You can also choose a mandala coloring book, coloring page, or grab chalk and color the sidewalk. Whatever method, the healing benefits remain (lowering anxiety and stress, stabilizing blood pressure) and you get closer to the moon!

Last Quarter Moon (also called Third Quarter)

The moon is half full. You're in the final stretch of the manifesting with the new moon cycle. This is the waning period as the moon decreases on its way to completing her cycle. The last quarter moon for every month is listed later within this section, as well as in the month-at-a-glance section.

This is a powerful time to take action on refining, adjusting and releasing. Breaking-free from negative thinking or worries is especially easy during this time as you flow with the pull from the waning moon.

Assess your progress. Identify any necessary changes. Release what is no longer supporting your manifesting desires.

This is a good time to discover if we've become out of sync somewhere. Notice any physical, emotional and spiritual imbalances. Maybe you're resenting giving so much time and energy into your dreams. Maybe you're losing confidence. Maybe you physically need some rest. This is the time to get refocused and re-establish balance. Investing in a fresh approach will infuse new energy and excitement into your new moon intention.

REFRESH

Investing in re-energizing yourself will invigorate your whole being. Here's a list of ways to perk your energy and your soul so you can assess your manifesting through a fresh lens.

- Get outdoors and appreciate the view.
- Call a friend and laugh. No business talk, just enjoying each other's company.
- Give yourself a hug
- Hug a pet
- Hug a friend
- Stretch
- Drink some water
- Eat chocolate
- Sing a song
- Dance
- Turn on lights. Better yet, get in the sunshine.
- Blow bubbles
- Skip
- Smell an orange or lemon
- Smile
- Breathe

THE DAY BEFORE NEXT NEW MOON

This is also referred to at the Dark Moon. It makes sense since the sky is dark. There's not even a glimmer of the moon. This is the easiest day of all.

Do nothing. Rest. Relax.

Moon Cycle Manifesting Guidesheet

New Moon

New Moon is the initial time for manifesting. It's a time of foundation, new groundwork, new excitement, energy, and belief.

Each cycle is divided into 8-minute sections.

Set aside 8 minutes.

STEP 1 – FOCUS

Set your timer for 30 seconds

Relax. Remove distractions. Set your timer. Close your eyes and relax. As you relax for 1 minute bring your attention to one sound. When thoughts slip in, simply acknowledge them and return your attention to the sound. Release any tension through your body, especially your jaw, shoulders, hands and feet. Breathe.

STEP 2 – DECIDE

Set your timer for 2 minutes

Decide 1 - 5 areas where you'd like new energy, new beginnings, new guidance, new starts, renewed strength. Consider the new moon's current astrological sign. Could you apply any of its specialties? Finish by asking yourself, "Is there anything else I'm ready to manifest at this time?" You may feel *nope, all good* or you may be surprised at the new insights revealed.

Here are some ideas to get you thinking.

new financial blessings	new projects
new clients	new social life
new love	new attitude
new exercise commitment	new excitement
renewed relationship	renewed strength
new self-care	new hope
new spiritual awakening	new ideas
new income	new home
new friendships	new car

STEP 3 – VISUALIZE

Set your timer for 2 minutes

From your notes above, begin visualizing every desire you just wrote has manifested. Lean into the excitement, happiness, and joy of this manifested reality. Really feel the positive emotions. Smile, do a happy dance. Get into this celebration!

STEP 4 – AFFIRMATION

Set your timer for 2 minutes

Write affirmations to support each of the desires manifested. Keep them positive and in the present tense. "Money constantly flows to me." Or "My body is healthy and whole."

You can also begin with "I am." For example, "I am loving my brand new convertible" or "I am a manifesting magnet."

STEP 5 – GRATITUDE

Set the timer for 30 seconds or skip the timer and go as long as you'd like.

Being grateful comes with a lot of health benefits. It also carries a lot of manifesting benefits. When you express your gratitude aloud you become a magnet for more things to be grateful for. Seriously. How cool is that?

You speak out thanking being grateful for this great day, having your dreams come true and your vibration just escalated on the manifesting scale. You are a noticeably beaming. A shining star. Then, you state your affirmation. It's positive, filled with present tense and you're offering gratitude for the affirmation you just stated. The universe hears you and is like, "Uh-oh, did I forget to give that to her? Eeeek! I've got to get right on that!"

When you're sharing your gratitude with the universe, be sure to include, "I'm so grateful for (this) or something better." Sometimes you underestimate the treasures that are just waiting for you to receive them. The "or something better" allows the "more" to come to you.

Know that what you've written has been added to the natural Law of Rhythm.

STEP 6 – EMBRACE

Set the timer for 1 minute

Smile. Spend one minute feeling confident in your outcome.

For as the moon is illuminated so shall it be.

First Quarter Moon

First Quarter Moon is the time for manifesting action steps.

Grab your New Moon Intention Worksheet and have it handy for this section.

STEP 1 – GROUND AND CENTER

Sit comfortably with feet flat on floor. Relax. Remove distractions. Set your timer. Close your eyes and relax. As you relax for 1 minute, bring your attention to one sound. When thoughts slip in, simply acknowledge them and return your attention to the sound. Release any tension through your body, especially your jaw, shoulders, hands and feet. Breathe.

STEP 2 – RECONNECT

Review your intentions, affirmations. What else can you be doing? Do you need blinders and earmuffs to tune out any negativity or distractions? Are you needing to jazz up your affirmations? Exhaustion and defeat can try to slip in so stay strong!

STEP 3 – RECOMMIT

Make a deal with yourself. At the top of your page write out your steps. Include this section at the bottom and sign and date.

I, [name], commit to taking the action steps I intuitively know to take. I will say my affirmations daily. I will spend _____ time visualizing this has manifested. I will keep my thoughts focused on the outcome I desire and only on the outcome of this or something better manifested.
Sign
Date

Full Moon

Large, bright, and round. This is invigorating. The full moon is offering total clarity on your new moon intentions.

Review Your New Moon Intention Sheet

Review your progress. Are any adjustments needed?

Physically – Take inventory of your actions. What's working? What isn't? What can you do to realign with your enthusiasm to this manifestation?

Emotionally – How are you feeling? Anxious? Bitter? Excited? Encouraged? Is there a theme your emotions are revealing?

Spiritually – Are you feeling the divine connection? Have you been trusting your intuition? This is a perfect opportunity to reconnect or strengthen the divine connection you already have.

Look over your general assessment of this month's progress. Take a cleansing breath as you see your paper. Don't let this be a time where you're beating yourself up. CELEBRATE everything you did right! I want hear the cheer even if you only said part of your affirmations. Cheer, even if you forgot all about your new moon intentions. Cheer that you woke up and shared your light with this world. This full moon is a time to fill with gratitude and let it overflow.

A special time of celebrations is cake and candles. You can make your own, buy one, or even skip the cake. Don't skip the candle though!

Grab a birthday candle. White, gold, pink, or blue are all great choices. Place in the cake or even hold it.

Prior to lighting, visualize your dream fulfilled. Imagine it has truly manifested. It feels so great doesn't it?

Any pings of negativity popping in? Any doubts? Could've or should'ves crossing your mind. That's okay.

Visualize your new moon intention manifested.

Light your candle.

You can sing this to the tune of Happy Birthday –

I am manifesting with the moon.
All my dreams do come true.
I have so much to celebrate....
I'm a manifestor, how 'bout you?

Blow out your candle. Safely dispose your candle and enjoy your cake! I know the song seems silly, but did you find yourself relaxing and maybe even smiling? That's the energy for manifesting! And, now you're doing it with the Moon Goddess joining you! How awesome is that?!

An aside... candles and cake dates back to Ancient Greece. A round cake (representing the moon) with candles on top were offered in celebration of the moon goddess, Artemis. The smoke from the candles would take the wishes, prayers and requests to the heavens. Talk about engaging with some additional manifesting help!

If cake and singing is not your cup of tea, here's a more conservative approach. No singing, but you can make up your own tune if you want!

Light your candle and state,

"I light this candle with the flame so bright.
Just like the moon, we are one with the light.
Dreams come true. I see it in my sight.
I manifest what I want and I know I am right."

Last Quarter Moon (also called Third Quarter)

The moon is half full. You're in the final stretch of the manifesting with the new moon cycle. This is the waning period as the moon decreases on its way to completing her cycle. The last quarter moon for every month is listed later within this section, as well as in the month-at-a-glance section.

This is one of my favorite times. It's like when you're doing a "spring cleaning" except it's with your cluttered thoughts, and action plans that have holes in them. You're emotionally and physically ready to toss them out.

This is usually that time when you're able to engage angels and be completely open to their ideas. This is where you really do embrace the "this or something better."

ANGEL TOOL

This has been one of the most powerful and magical manifesting tools for me, my children, friends, and clients. I really know this will be for you too!

On a fresh piece of paper draw a vertical line down the center of the page. Draw a horizontal line at the top of the page about 2 inches or 5 centimeters. This does not have to be perfect.

At the top of the left column write, "Angels." At the top of the right column write, "Me."

Write your angel to-do list. Write everything you want them to handle. Everything. All of your manifesting dreams. Those items from your New Moon Intention sheet goes in that angel column. Give it all to the angels.

For your column, write what you want to control. Items could include smiling, staying in the positive vibration, guarding your thoughts, and trusting your intuition. Remember, you are not to include the things you just gave to the angels.

When your list is complete, carry it around, place it at the side of your bed, take a photo and make it your wallpaper on your phone. It's important to not sneak in and take the manifesting duties from your angels. They've got this! And so do you!

Moon Cycles for 2022

Every month's moon cycle brings unique energy to manifesting. However, don't get tripped up thinking you can't manifest anything unless it's during the New Moon. You can manifest anything at any time.

These are guidelines for working with the energy of every moon in 2022. Always, trust your intuition. You know yourself best!

All the days and times are listed as US Eastern Time. Please check for your local time. I like the website https://www.timeanddate.com/moon/phases/

Moon dates listed with an * are simply to remind you to pay attention. It may be a supermoon. It may be that the new moon straddles two days – depending on your time zone. It may be an eclipse or some other planetary movement. Just pay attention.

SOME THINGS TO NOTE

- At the end of March and the beginning of April, the New Moon cycle begins to shift into the previous month. When the moon straddles a day, plant your New Moon manifesting intentions on the later date.

- There are several supermoons. Please add these to your phone calendars and set reminders. These are powerful and fortuitous manifesting moments.

- There are several eclipses. Please, also add these to your schedule. These bring swift and successful manifesting change. (This begins a new chapter and needs to begin on right side of page.)

January Moon Cycle

———

MANIFESTING ENERGY
New Beginnings, New Starts,
New Theme

FULL MOON IN CANCER
17 Jan 6:48 pm

NEW MOON IN CAPRICORN*
Supermoon
2 January 1:33 pm

LAST QUARTER
25 Jan 8:40 am

NEW MOON IN AQUARIUS*
1 February 12:46 am

FIRST QUARTER
9 Jan 1:11 pm

Tips for manifesting with this New Supermoon in Capricorn

The Supermoon is brighter and larger due to its current orbit. This impacts emotions and manifesting energies. Be open to your dreams coming true. If you knew you would receive it, what would you ask for? That's this energy flowing right now!

Capricorn brings the energy of accomplishing that mountain that's been so difficult to climb. She's got the focus, schedule, and fortitude to achieve anything she puts her mind to. Hardworking, self-reliant, and practical, Capricorn is the goat which is the symbol of abundance, fertility, and good luck. What new seeds do you want to plant in this fertile cosmic soil, because Capricorn is going to lend her energy and confidence to accomplish it.

Tips for manifesting with this Full Moon in Cancer

This is a truly magical time. Cancer is ruled by the moon. Having the moon in her sign amplifies her magical gifts. Cancer brings the nurturing energy of the goddess. Use this full moon for manifesting things of the home, family, and love. Trust your intuition. Cancer, emotional and highly intuitive, will bring greater insight if you will trust her guidance.

Tips for manifesting with this New Moon in Aquarius

Depending on your time zone, there will be NO new moon in your area for the month of February as it may occur on January 31. This is significant. This occurs every 19 years. In numerology, the 1 brings the energy of wholeness, new beginning, your soul. The 9 represent a completed cycle. Think back 19 years ago. What were you doing? What did you want? What dreams have manifested in that time? What dreams have you forgotten? What new dreams were birthed from this time? What new beginnings would you like to infuse into this New Moon cycle? This will be a powerful manifesting new cycle wherever you're celebrating this New Moon.

Aquarius brings the energy of independence, freedom, and quirkiness. This creates the freedom and confidence to manifest what you truly desire. No judgements or outside opinions will sway you. This is a great time to plant seeds for unique opportunities, changing an old routine, welcoming new dynamics in love, and taking action in releasing emotional limitations and emotions.

February Moon Cycle

MANIFESTING ENERGY
Mystical, Loving, Partnerships

NEW MOON IN AQUARIUS*
1 February 12:46 am

FIRST QUARTER
8 February 8:50 am

FULL MOON IN LEO
16 February 11:56 am

LAST QUARTER
23 February 5:32 pm

Tips for manifesting with this New Moon in Aquarius

Depending on your time zone, there will be NO new moon in your area
for the month of February as it may occur on January 31. This is significant. This occurs every 19 years. In numerology, the 1 brings the energy
of wholeness, new beginning, your soul. The 9 represent a completed
cycle. Think back 19 years ago. What were you doing? What did you
want? What dreams have manifested in that time? What dreams have
you forgotten? What new dreams were birthed from this time? What
new beginnings would you like to infuse into this New Moon cycle? This
will be a powerful manifesting new cycle wherever you're celebrating
this New Moon.

Aquarius brings the energy of independence, freedom, and quirkiness. This creates the freedom and confidence to manifest what you truly desire. No judgements or outside opinions will sway you. This is a great time to plant seeds for unique opportunities, changing an old routine, welcoming new dynamics in love, and taking action in releasing emotional limitations and emotions.

Tips for manifesting with this Full Moon in Leo

Leo has a natural magnetism. They stand out in a crowd with beautiful energy and an engaging confidence. They're noticed. Your dreams will be too! Look for this Full Moon to reveal what has been fulfilled from your New Moon intentions and roar your gratitude! Leo's lion will help you maintain patience as you're manifesting your new moon desires.

March Moon Cycle

MANIFESTING ENERGY
Powerful & Gentle, Good Luck,
Swift Shifts

FULL MOON IN VIRGO
18 March 3:17 am

NEW MOON IN PISCES
2 March 12:34 pm

LAST QUARTER
25 March 1:37 am

FIRST QUARTER
10 March 5:45 am

NEW MOON IN ARIES*
1 April 2:24 am

Tips for manifesting with this New Moon in Pisces

Pisces brings her gifts of intuition, sensitivity, creativity, and compassion. You'll be able to go for what you truly desire and know that you are worthy of this. Implement elements of art into your new moon intentions. For example, journal your new moon desires and then add doodles and splashes of color around it. You're directing the manifesting energies. This is a great time for manifesting an abundant flow of love in your personal and work life.

Tips for manifesting with this Full Moon in Virgo

This is a productive time! Virgo brings the structure, organization and planning. She'll help you identify and easily release what isn't working. She'll then assist you in creating a detailed to-do list for manifesting action steps to be completed prior to the next new moon. Virgo is efficient and kind. Let her show you the way.

Tips for manifesting with this New Moon in Aries

This is one of those occasions where some will have the New Moon the day before. You can set your New Moon intentions either day.

Aries brings the optimism, confidence, and energy to manifest what you want. Its childlike faith and spirit will help you have the aligned attitude and emotions for manifesting. Aries will help you stay brave, so this is an optimal time for taking risks. Remember that thing you gave up on? This is the time to go for it and let the New Moon in Aries spring the manifesting energy into action.

April Moon Cycle

———

MANIFESTING ENERGY
Beauty, Love, Fertility

FULL MOON IN LIBRA
16 April 2:55 pm

NEW MOON IN ARIES*
1 April 2:24 am

LAST QUARTER
23 April 7:56 am

FIRST QUARTER
9 April 2:47 am

NEW MOON IN TAURUS*
Solar Eclipse
30 April 4:28 pm

Tips for manifesting with this New Moon in Aries

This is one of those occasions where some will have the New Moon the day before. You can set your New Moon intentions either day.

Aries brings the optimism, confidence, and energy to manifest what you want. Its childlike faith and spirit will help you have the aligned attitude and emotions for manifesting. Aries will help you stay brave, so this is an optimal time for taking risks. Remember that thing you gave up on? This is the time to go for it and let the New Moon in Aries spring the manifesting energy into action.

Tips for manifesting with this Full Moon in Libra

Libra brings the balance. Where are things lopsided in your manifesting? This is a time to check for areas that are holding you back. Use this Full Moon to reveal what you've been thinking, saying and feeling. Anything not in line with manifesting success can be immediately adjusted. Libra is ruled by Venus so any changes and revelations will be shared with love.

Tips for manifesting with this New Moon in Taurus

This new moon coincides with a solar eclipse. Mark your calendar and use this energy wisely.

This solar eclipse is a partial one. But don't be fooled by the word, partial. It's still going to give all energy of a full solar eclipse.

Solar eclipses influence the outer... taking action, impacting outward change, manifesting outward abundance. Eclipses brings swift and powerful change. Wish wisely!

A solar eclipse has more masculine energy. This is perfect for taking fast action and engaging in the manifesting energy. Taurus has abundant divine feminine energy. She brings beauty, determination, and endurance. This is a beautiful blend of time to plant the seeds of prosperity and wealth. This graceful Goddess Venus has friends in high places and will call on them to assist in your manifesting. Trust your intuition and take immediate action. You are in the Divine flow!

May Moon Cycle

MANIFESTING ENERGY
Fertility, Celebration, Blooming

NEW MOON IN TAURUS*
Solar Eclipse
Cycle began
30 April 4:28 pm

FIRST QUARTER
8 May 8:21 pm

FULL MOON IN SCORPIO
Lunar Eclipse
16 May 12:14

LAST QUARTER
22 May 2:43 pm

NEW MOON IN GEMINI
30 May 7:30 am

Tips for manifesting with this New Moon in Taurus

This new moon coincides with a solar eclipse. Mark your calendar and use this energy wisely.

This solar eclipse is a partial one. But don't be fooled by the word, partial. It's still going to give all energy of a full solar eclipse.

Solar eclipses influence the outer... taking action, impacting outward change, manifesting outward abundance. Eclipses brings swift and powerful change. Wish wisely!

A solar eclipse has more masculine energy. This is perfect for taking fast action and engaging in the manifesting energy. Taurus has abundant divine feminine energy. She brings beauty, determination, and endurance. This is a beautiful blend of time to plant the seeds of prosperity and wealth. This graceful Goddess Venus has friends in high places and will call on them to assist in your manifesting. Trust your intuition and take immediate action. You are in the Divine flow!

Tips for manifesting with this Full Moon in Scorpio

This is also a total Lunar Eclipse. The Lunar influences the inner... trusting intuition, impacting inner change, manifesting emotional breakthroughs. Eclipses brings swift and powerful change. Use it wisely.

This lunar eclipse will go deep into your emotions and divine feminine energy. This is the time to reveal where you may not be honoring your gifts, your intuition, your uniqueness. Scorpio brings the vulnerability so you can open up and no longer hide. Your dreams are worth being manifested. If you're feeling unworthy in a small area, then the big yearnings are going to be more difficult to manifest. Let this full moon do its thing. Point out the blockage and make the correction so you can manifest what you're passionate about.

Tips for manifesting with this New Moon in Gemini

Gemini lends it's flirty, fun and spontaneous energy to this New Moon. Gemini is quick to blurt, so she'll help you promptly identify exactly what you want. And, there is no issue with communication so write down your heart's desire! The universe is ready to boost your energy and power. Gemini energy is swift, so quickly jot your New Moon intentions down and let the manifesting fun begin.

June Moon Cycle

MANIFESTING ENERGY
Vitality, Romance, Joy

FULL MOON IN SAGITTARIUS*
Supermoon
14 June 7:51 am

NEW MOON IN GEMINI*
Cycle began
30 May 7:30 am

LAST QUARTER
20 June 11:10 pm

FIRST QUARTER
7 June 10:48

NEW MOON IN CANCER*
28 June 10:52 pm

Tips for manifesting with this New Moon in Gemini

Gemini lends it's flirty, fun and spontaneous energy to this New Moon. Gemini is quick to blurt, so she'll help you promptly identify exactly what you want. And, there is no issue with communication so write down your heart's desire! The universe is ready to boost your energy and power. Gemini energy is swift, so quickly jot your New Moon intentions down and let the manifesting fun begin.

Tips for manifesting with this Full Supermoon in Sagittarius

While the energy is amplified, so will the emotions. Sagittarius is perfect for seeing your manifesting seeds through to fruition. She complements Gemini. Both communicators, Sag is going to bring enthusiasm and optimism to this Supermoon. She'll also raise your intuition to show you any needed steps for manifesting. Sagittarius is honest and will just tell you straight up. She loves education, so don't be surprised if she suggests classes. This powerful manifesting moon contains so much magic. Grab your journal and ask for clarity under this wise, full supermoon light.

Tips for manifesting with this New Moon in Cancer

The moon rules Cancer so they're going to tag team to help nurture, protect, and sprout your New Moon intentions. We just experienced a major balancing shift with the solstice. Intuitively ask yourself what you want to truly manifest. We're approaching the Sirius Gateway which opens doors widely to independence and freedom. This would be the time to integrate those aspects, if you desire, into your New Moon intentions.

July Moon Cycle

———

MANIFESTING ENERGY
Independence, Spiritual,
Personal Power

FULL MOON IN CAPRICORN*
Supermoon
13 July 2:37 pm

NEW MOON IN CANCER*
Cycle began
28 June 10:52 pm

LAST QUARTER
20 July 10:18 am

FIRST QUARTER
6 July 10:14 pm

NEW MOON IN LEO
28 July 1:54 pm

Tips for manifesting with this New Moon in Cancer

The moon rules Cancer so they're going to tag team to help nurture, protect, and sprout your New Moon intentions. We just experienced a major balancing shift with the solstice. Intuitively ask yourself what you want to truly manifest. We're approaching the Sirius Gateway which opens doors widely to independence and freedom. This would be the time to integrate those aspects, if you desire, into your New Moon intentions.

Tips for manifesting with this Full Supermoon in Capricorn

Energy is amplified and so are emotions. Plus, this Supermoon is following the spiritual boost from the Sirius Gateway. You intuitively know that you're a diving being, able to manifest your dreams. Capricorn will take this to a new level. Stubborn, she will not allow this dream to fizzle out. Capricorn brings the cornucopia, the symbol of abundance. She's intelligent and will help you navigate the next steps to swiftly manifest your dreams.

Tips for manifesting with this New Moon in Leo

Leo is going to help you take action on anything you plant during your New Moon intention. Where do you want center stage? Where do you want to exude confidence? This New Moon intention holds the key. Write down all the areas where you want the manifesting attention. Then, connect with Leo's confidence. You'll find the manifesting doors opening with the warmth and love of the sun.

August Moon Cycle

MANIFESTING ENERGY
Manifesting, Harvest, Gratitude

FULL MOON IN AQUARIUS
11 August 9:35 pm

NEW MOON IN LEO*
Cycle began
28 July 1:54 pm

LAST QUARTER
19 August 12:36 am

FIRST QUARTER
5 August 7:06 am

NEW MOON IN VIRGO
27 August 4:17 am

Tips for manifesting with this New Moon in Leo

Leo is going to help you take action on anything you plant during your New Moon intention. Where do you want center stage? Where do you want to exude confidence? This New Moon intention holds the key. Write down all the areas where you want the manifesting attention. Then, connect with Leo's confidence. You'll find the manifesting doors opening with the warmth and love of the sun.

Tips for manifesting with this Full Moon in Aquarius

This full moon in the air sign Aquarius will fuel the manifesting fire that Leo lit during your New Moon intentions and the powerful manifesting energy from the Lionsgate Portal on 8th of August. While, if you connected, you're probably still feeling in the flow. If you forgot or didn't notice, that's okay, you're still sensing the manifesting increased frequency.

Aquarius will share her opinions and guidance under this Full Moon to ensure you're on the right track. Anything left to question, needed shifts, or adjustments, Aquarius will provide insight. She'll most likely pour out unconventional ways to attract, release, and celebrate. Be open during this Full Moon as insight doesn't just trickle, it flows. Be poised to take action. You'll have much to celebrate by September.

Tips for manifesting with this New Moon in Virgo

Virgo is a minimalist, detail-oriented, a perfectionist. She will help create the perfect New Moon intention for this manifesting cycle. September is a month of completion. Virgo will guide you in every step needed to communicate, organize, and transform your New Moon intention. Efficient and able to achieve all she sets out to achieve, Virgo is a manifesting goddess.

September Moon Cycle

MANIFESTING ENERGY
Goddess Energy,
Transformation, Growth

FULL MOON IN PISCES
10 September 5:59 am

NEW MOON VIRGO*
Cycle began
27 August 4:17 am

LAST QUARTER
17 September 5:52 pm

FIRST QUARTER
3 September 2:07 pm

NEW MOON IN LIBRA
25 September 5:54 pm

Tips for manifesting with this New Moon in Virgo

Virgo is a minimalist, detail-oriented, a perfectionist. She will help create the perfect New Moon intention for this manifesting cycle. September is a month of completion. Virgo will guide you in every step needed to communicate, organize, and transform your New Moon intention. Efficient and able to achieve all she sets out to achieve, Virgo is a manifesting goddess.

Tips for manifesting with this Full Moon in Pisces

Sensitive, creative and intuitive, Pisces shares her incredible wisdom to this Full Moon. This would be a great time to soak in the tub, relax in the shower or sit under the Full Moon sky and bathe in the light and loving energy. Ask for any insight, subtle shifts needed or anything needing changed so your New Moon intentions can be manifested easier. Pisces may communicate through a song, piece of art or to just stay in the flow. Either way, she is sensitive to your needs. And, don't be surprised if she subtly suggests working with spirit guides during this time.

Tips for manifesting with this New Moon in Libra

This New Moon is following the surge of manifesting energy created from the recent Equinox.

Equinox brings balance and so does Libra! What timing! Use this New Moon to offer setting the energy straight in your manifesting. Are there areas where things seem lopsided? Are you seeking balance in any area of your life? New Moon in Libra is perfect for creating balance in all of your relationships and within yourself. Libra is ruled by Venus, so tap into the energies of beauty, money, and love when setting your New Moon intentions.

October Moon Cycle

———

MANIFESTING ENERGY
Magical, New Beginnings &
Endings, Manifesting

NEW MOON IN LIBRA*
Cycle began
25 September 5:54 pm

FIRST QUARTER
2 October 8:14 pm

FULL MOON IN ARIES
9 October 4:54 pm

LAST QUARTER
17 October 1:15 pm

NEW MOON IN SCORPIO*
Solar Eclipse
25 October 6:48 am

Tips for manifesting with this New Moon in Libra

This New Moon is following the surge of manifesting energy created from the recent Equinox.

Equinox brings balance and so does Libra! What timing! Use this New Moon to offer setting the energy straight in your manifesting. Are there areas where things seem lopsided? Are you seeking balance in any area of your life? New Moon in Libra is perfect for creating balance in all of your relationships and within yourself. Libra is ruled by Venus, so tap into the energies of beauty, money and love when setting your New Moon intentions.

Tips for manifesting with this Full Moon in Aries

Your New Moon intentions were positioned in fertile manifesting soil. Now, this Full Moon is positioned right before a powerful manifesting day of 10/10. October has overflowing manifesting energy. This Full Moon in Aries will reveal much, including how to stay strong and determined. You'll probably also glean insight into new and original ways of manifesting your intentions. Aries is ruled by Mars and will help complete this cycle.

Tips for manifesting with this New Moon in Scorpio

This New Moon is following the surge of manifesting energy created from the recent Solar Eclipse.

Eclipses brings swift change. The Solar Eclipse inspires action. What a great foundation for this New Moon in Scorpio. Passionate, intuitive, and energetic, Scorpio has just the right vibe to plant the seeds you want manifested. Utilize Scorpio's strong drive to dig deep and hone in on the divine and intuitive messages provided from your angels, spirit guides, and the universe. You'll position yourself to succeed, often before the Full Moon!

November Moon Cycle

——

MANIFESTING ENERGY
Gratitude, Angels, Abundance

NEW MOON IN SCORPIO*
Cycle began
25 October 6:48 am

FIRST QUARTER
1 November 2:37 am

FULL MOON IN TAURUS*
Lunar Eclipse
8 November 6:02 am

LAST QUARTER
16 November 8:27 am

NEW MOON IN SAGITTARIUS
23 November 5:57 pm

Tips for manifesting with this New Moon in Scorpio

This New Moon is following the surge of manifesting energy created from the recent Solar Eclipse.

Eclipse brings swift change. Solar Eclipse inspires action. What a great foundation for this New Moon in Scorpio. Passionate, intuitive and energetic, Scorpio has just the right vibe to plant the seeds you want manifested. Utilize Scorpio's strong drive to dig deep and hone in on the divine messages and intuitive messages provided from your angels, spirit guides and the universe. You'll position yourself to succeed, often before the Full Moon!

Tips for manifesting with this Full Moon in Taurus

Ooooh this is so magical! The 8 brings the manifesting energy and the 11 brings the angel's energy. Taurus, ruled by Venus, brings the goddess energy and so does the moon. This is a powerful time to step into your divine gifts. You are a divine being, a co-creator of your life. Use this Full Moon to reveal needed steps to own your power. You are a natural manifestor. Clarity and guidance is realized with this magical and beautiful Full Moon.

Tips for manifesting with this New Moon in Sagittarius

Sagittarius loves to expand her horizon and this New Moon is perfect timing. She will help you dream outside of your comfort zone. This is a homestretch of 2022. Sagittarius provides the energy and hope to see your dreams manifested. Ruled by Jupiter, Sagittarius has the intimate connection with the planet that likes to shower you with manifesting your dreams. This is beyond a glass half full time, this is an overflowing of magical, manifesting energy time!

December Moon Cycle

———

MANIFESTING ENERGY
Divine Guidance, Vibrational
Increase, Transformation

NEW MOON IN SAGITTARIUS*
Cycle began
23 November 5:57 pm

FIRST QUARTER
30 November 9:36 am

FULL MOON IN GEMINI
7 December 11:08 pm

LAST QUARTER
16 December 3:56 am

NEW MOON IN CAPRICORN*
Supermoon
23 December 5:16 am

FIRST QUARTER
29 December 8:20 pm

Tips for manifesting with this New Moon in Sagittarius

Sagittarius loves to expand her horizon and this New Moon is perfect timing. She will help you dream outside of your comfort zone. This is a homestretch of 2022. Sagittarius provides the energy and hope to see your dreams manifested. Ruled by Jupiter, Sagittarius has the intimate connection with the planet that likes to shower you with manifesting your dreams. This is beyond a glass half full time, this is an overflowing of magical, manifesting energy time!

Tips for manifesting with this Full Moon in Gemini

This is the perfect time to freshen up that New Moon Intention list. Look it over and intuitively connect with changes that need to be made. Sagittarius energy will help Gemini energy focus, hone in, and instinctually know the best course of action to take for your happily ever after. This is a Full Moon ready for full transformation.

Tips for manifesting with this New Supermoon in Capricorn

We just had the Solstice. That provides an energetic shift. There's more of an opening with your angels guiding you. This is prime for setting what you want to manifest into the new year!

And, it just keeps getting better! This is a Supermoon. This impacts emotions and manifesting energies. Be open to your dreams coming true. If you knew you would receive it, what would you ask for? That's this energy flowing right now!

Capricorn brings the energy of accomplishing that mountain that's been so difficult to climb. She's got the focus, schedule, and fortitude to achieve anything she puts her mind to. Hardworking, self-reliant, and practical, Capricorn is the goat which is the symbol of abundance, fertility and good luck. Think about what new seeds you want to plant in this fertile cosmic soil, because Capricorn is going to lend her energy, determination and confidence.

Manifesting is a magical journey.

★

*And definitely more fun when shared
with the cosmic helpers.*

*Continue working with your cosmic family
and continue manifesting,
because the more you manifest. . .
the more you manifest!*

ABOUT THE AUTHOR

Trish McKinnley is a spiritual lifestyle and manifesting expert who's passionate about helping your dreams become a reality. Creator of Goddessology® and The Forgotten Tools of the Universe, Trish is known around the world for her cosmic intuition on guardians, angels, fairies, crystals, and how to live an effortlessly spiritual and fabulous life.

Named Soul & Spirit magazine's "Rising Star," Trish can be found enjoying her manifested happily ever after, complete with modern-day castle and handsome prince... a remarkable manifestation for a single mom with six kids!

WWW.TRISHMCKINNLEY.COM

WWW.ESSENTIALMANIFESTINGGUIDEBOOK.COM

Printed in Great Britain
by Amazon